AMERICAN OAK FURNITURE

BOOK II

Kathryn McNerney

cb

COLLECTOR BOOKS
A Division of Schroeder Publishing Co., Inc.

Cover photo: solid oak table, glass ball feet held by four-prong metal talons. 30"h x 28"sq. Shelf is 19"sq x 10"h from floor. $365.00.

Searching For A Publisher?

We are always looking for knowledgeable people considered to be experts within their fields. If you feel that there is a real need for a book on your collectible subject and have a large comprehensive collection, contact us.

COLLECTOR BOOKS
P.O. Box 3009
Paducah, Kentucky 42002-3009

Cover design by Beth Summers
Book design by Gina Lage

Additional copies of this book may be ordered from:

Collector Books
P.O. Box 3009
Paducah, Kentucky 42002-3009

@ $12.95. Add $2.00 for postage and handling.

Printed by Inland Press.

FOR MY SON TOM

Appreciation

To dealers, exhibitors and managers in shows and malls, and many others no longer in open shops:

"Thank You!"...only two small words, but none can more fully express my deep gratitude for the help you've given me with pictures and information; for the pleasure of knowing you, your hospitality and your courtesies. And lest we forget: Debbie Mize, Bettie Hewett, Nettie Stimson, Steve and Joan Fellows, and my Happy Toter and Gofer Sharon Fisher, for the fun we had, and your patience.

Florida

Fernandina Beach
Amelia Antique Market
Eight Flags Antique Mall
Rosanna Oliver

Jacksonville
Avondale Antique Mall
Bayard Country Store
The Lamp Post, Inc.

Jacksonville Beach
Beaches Antique Gallery

Orange Park
B & D Antiques
Brian Tebo
Ladybug Antiques and
Collectibles
Mr. and Mrs. Robert George
The David Bells
Timely Treasures

Georgia

Cave Spring
Country Roads Antique Mall

Rome
Ozment Antique Gallery

New York

Clarence
Clarence Antique World
Clarence Exposition
Ruth's Antiques, Inc.
The Muleskinner

Leroy
Vintage Antique Center

Lewiston
Lexington Square
Stimson's Antiques and Gifts

Lockport
A Festival of Antiques at
Kenan Center

Contents

Abbreviations

ca	circa – about the time of
bk	back
dia	diameter
dp	deep
ea	each
fl	floor – height up from
frt	front
h	height
l	length
pr	pair
rd	round
ref	refinished
res	restored
sp	spelling
w	width

Furniture herein is principally from the nineteenth century, with other time periods noted. Many objects flow on into the twentieth century. This is a report of articles tagged for sale by dealers, and articles in collections given a certain value by their owners. Each piece is in fine or mint condition, having been refinished/restored if necessary.

The Oak

Timeless Symbol of Generous Strength

With "Forest to Furniture" detailed in Book I as "Source, Woods, Making, Sales, Values, and Nice to Know," herein research is extended. During my first manuscript-interview years ago at Collector Books, it was stipulated that I always write to "make sense." And so, skirting tedious repetition insofar as possible, background references to those previous topics are to better "make sense." Also introduced in Book I was an apprehensive acorn gale-pitched from its home-bough onto a spongy earth-mat below.

And now Book II...reassured by the heartening concern of his anxious white oak parent, the little brown rounded nut stopped shaking. And he listened as the quavery rustlings from the autumn foliage above whispered on: "At least 300 species of our extended families comprise the Beech genus, divided into two groups. Ours, of smooth-lobe leaves, is most important to hardwood industries. The other, the black (or red) is spike-lobed. Sometimes a timber chestnut is included, along with suitable ash, elm, even hickory trees. Native largely to north temperate climes, tropical oaks are mainly evergreens. We are more resistant to the voracious powder post beetles than most other woods (as the susceptible lighter-weight chestnut ravaged in 1870 by an Asian Blight). As timber oak we are very tough and durable, odorless, fast-growing, and coarse-grained, this last accentuated by rapid maturing. Experienced woodsmen may have grown accustomed to seeing our unusual surface finishes revealed when trees are felled. But novice lumberjacks would be amazed at unexpected surprises! Quarters cut lengthwise — from heart to bark — are known as wood "quarter-sawn" (or sawed). Thus exposed are a myriad of pith rays and color shadings, lovely wavy ribbons and swirls and thicker wriggley stripes. While this quartering proves more expensive due to its requiring larger logs, more handling, and an extravagant loss of wood, there is less shrinkage and warping — especially advantageous in building furniture."

Hearing all this the acorn rose, having come to terms with his fall in view of his great potential. Deeply anchoring roots into the soil, day by day he stretched toward a distant sky-patch, embracing heat and cold, sunshine and storms. Constantly changing his mind (as younguns do) it was fun to "imagine" being chosen to be carried out into the world and what he might become! Then, growing older, he relaxed, deciding to "let come what may" and at last, the whisperings were still.

One marvels at the historical significance of the oak. The whole tree, even its bark, has contributed to the economic, aesthetic, and social well-being of so many cultures throughout so many generations.

Revered since earliest known legends, the oak was sacred to Zeus. It was worshiped by the Druids; Germanic peoples honored it with a special day of observance, and it was prominent in medieval Europe.

A preferred furniture wood during the Gothic years, dark English oak (resembling American walnut) remained a favorite with the Jacobeans. In the seventeenth century American oak was popular on this continent. During the mid-1600s, a Massachusetts town found itself swamped under a trading boom. Despite a British ban against it, their general court hired a village silversmith who also worked in gold to mint additional coins in an effort to accelerate billings and currency exchanges. The Oaktree (note old spelling) was chosen as a design for some of the new shillings.

During the early 1700s, North American coastal ports built hundreds of ships from white oak, at times combining it with pine and spruce. In those years lumber mills, close to seemingly inexhaustible ancient forests, supplied very long, very wide planks needed for ships and framings for Colonial homes. The builder's technique of making mortised joints stronger by driving wooden pins through them was adapted by skilled craftsmen constructing heavy furniture.

With diminishing woodlands, timber oaks were smaller and less useful, although all kinds of builders, especially those of furniture, still demanded oak. Builders began to use other woods such as walnut, hickory, cherry, maple, and pine, with oak extensively applied for veneering and ornamentation. In the nineteenth century, furniture factories might print black ink on maple and such plainer woods, followed by staining for "the look of oak browns." Each maker had his own secret formula, intended to beautify and protect the finishes. There were about as many closely guarded "recipes" as there were furniture producers.

More and more factories were being established in cities from Canada to New Orleans and in the Far West. One concentration was at Grand Rapids, Michigan. Their growth climaxed as the Industrial Revolution circa 1860 – 1890, when our culture was transformed from agricultural to manufacturing and consumption. Although farming methods also advanced, industrialization in the cities swept ahead, and people moved into the towns. While expert cabinetmakers might still occasionally be hired for quality work on intricate embellishments, most formerly independent craftsmen, faced with having to keep food on their tables, were eventually absorbed into the Machine Age.

Beset by customers wanting purchases built and delivered yesterday, furniture manufacturers provided vast quantities of attractive and durable goods within the cost limits of many incomes. Orders came from affluent folks and from a surging middle class never dreaming they'd afford such "luxuries." Factories standardized dimensions for their wares, to be able to accommodate customers' room spaces and to ship pieces at the lowest possible cost.

Rival makers traded, surreptitiously copied, or simply took each other's most popular styles. Pictures herein did not appear in Book I. Nevertheless, when innumerable factories were turning out endless pieces, there were bound to be "similars" and "look alikes," especially chairs. Some might have been made from the same patterns.

"Catalog Fashions" thrived in the late 1800s. The foremost mail order houses — Sears Roebuck, Eaton's of Canada, Montgomery Ward, and Larkin's — sent their catalogs everywhere: to cities and towns, isolated seacoast hamlets, remote farms and ranches, and to lonely crossroads general stores. Eagerly awaited copies arriving at central locations in sparsely populated areas soon had well-thumbed pages and tattered covers. With the arrival of a new copy, the old one wasn't tossed away — instead, pages might be torn out to line shelves, tacked up to brighten somber log and cottage walls, or crushed to help stuff mattresses. Sears' 1897 catalog contained over 780 pages.

A whole family might gather after supper round a table, the latest catalog ready for viewing, an oil lamp flickers at center, the freshly trimmed wick turned low as possible to avoid smoking its polished glass chimney (but still recklessly high enough to "see good by"). Leaning shoulder to shoulder, they slowly pass the thick, profusely illustrated book, glancing at the flipped-through pages. They confer, accepting Papa's final decisions on work and home necessities. Next they breathlessly watch Mama count for the "nth" time her saved-up egg and butter coins to see how far those could go toward exciting "extras." All that accomplished, everyone in turn slowly browses the pages, exclaiming over pictures of wonderful temptations they might be able to afford later on.

There was an additional "Special Furniture Catalog" customers might order if they could not find what they wanted in the general catalog. Therein chairs were among the most representative merchandise. Many factories, imitating the avidly-sought hand carving, might achieve that look pretty well by pressing heated metal dies into chair backs, thus embossing a design. Sometimes a slight hand carving might be included. At first, collectors snubbed these really fine quality chairs. Now "pressbacks" are appreciated and widely purchased. Side chairs were customarily intended as part of dining room sets; but more often than not, these sets today have only five chairs. One reason given is that through the years when a chair's part was broken, or overall it became too worn, the strong elements were removed to bolster a weakness in another chair, thus making a total of five good chairs.

At first furniture was sent to local agents for uncrating, repairs and/or adjustments before delivery to buyers. Soon purchases went direct to customers in a nineteenth century "do-it-yourself" method. Gustav Stickley promoted this idea. He was one of a family furniture making business in 1882 at Syracuse, New York. Bypassing mail order houses, he sent his smaller editions straight to consumers. He believed in self-expression through home furniture choices, and that there was pleasurable satisfaction in handwork (as related to the seeds he planted for the Arts and Crafts Movement of that time). Also, he wanted to simplify both furniture lines and sales costs.

Two Englishmen, William Morris and Charles Locke Eastlake, were a part of the Arts and Crafts Movement. Their ideas, too, were for simple styles. Arts and Crafts ideas were carried out by various American manufacturers, such as Elbert Hubbard, who established his business at Aurora, New York, upon leaving the Larkin Soap Manufacturing Co. at Buffalo, New York. He called his colony the Roycrofters. (Although making and selling soap remained their primary purpose, Larkin went on to become a huge furniture making empire. In my research, I found one couple who seeks only pieces made by Larkin's.)

In California the Greene Brothers adapted Oriental themes for their output. The Limbert Brothers Factory in 1893 was one of 62 furniture makers in Grand Rapids. Semi-annual markets were held there; 200 manufacturers were represented in 1908.

Enjoying a lively popularity at the turn of the twentieth century, golden oak finish today remains very popular. This color was achieved by sanding to open the pores and smooth roughness from the white wood; a hard orange shellac, sometimes with a yellow ochre pigment, was then added. Antique oak finish was sprayed around areas to be highlighted. Sometimes nut brown stains were used to effect a burn. A Florida dealer remarked recently that their shop is selling a surprising amount of oak furniture in nut brown stains. Fumed oak was not so popular. Light wood pieces sealed in an airtight room with nearby open containers of ammonia were darkened by the fumes. Weathered oak had a soft gray finish with a silvery sheen.

Oak has been an important furniture wood in America since the founding of the first colonies. Its popularity has gone through cycles — when oak trees were plentiful, oak furniture was popular and abundant. Then the supply of mature oak trees would be depleted, and manufacturers would use other woods as a new generation of oaks grew big enough to be turned into lumber.

In the early nineteenth century, the availablility of oak was decreasing and walnut furniture, effusively decorated in Victorian style, was gaining popularity. By the 1870's, forests further west became accessible to lumbermen while those oaks that had been saplings at the beginning of the Victorian era were finally large enough to cut down. The popularity of oak peaked once again in the 1880's, only to decline by the 1930's when the new oak supplies were depleted. Sixty to a hundred years after the last oak boom, we once again see mature oak trees being timbered, and oak as a furniture wood is once again among the leaders.

Today there is still fine original oak furniture in the marketplaces. Collectors searching for that "special treasure" may consider that the piece once found might be lost to another buyer should there be too much hesitation.

And other folks simply browse the antique furniture sources to enjoy and perhaps understand more about some of the things our ancestors placed inside bare walls to establish homes.

And in experiencing the aura of heritage as they view those intensely eloquent expressions of eras past, everyone is surely reminded of the endurance of that most remarkable tree — THE OAK.

Beds and Armoires

MURPHY BED
Dealer had tagged, along with the price, "Fantastic!" Careful attention given to large and varied designs in applied machine carvings; dull brass knobs and pulls; beveled mirror at the back of a deep recess with two drawers. The three lower middle drawers are only false fronts. The bed is held in a side-paneled rolled-base frame. 60"l x 54"w x 20"dp. $1,595.00.

One could enjoy this as a dining buffet or in a bed-room to hold small items.

SLEIGH BED
Ca. 1840; quarter-cut veneering at headboard and footboard; wood casters. Back 52"h. Base 45"h. $750.00.

BED
Head and foot boards wide paneled; applied machine carvings; heavy crest. One dealer advised that when storing beds "casters should always be removed or the bed would begin to tilt." Hung over the base is a factory-made coverlet in an old pattern. Baseboard 33"h. Headboard 76"h x 56½"w. $500.00.

BED
Eastlake style in oak and maple. This has been cut down to a more convenient size to fit available space in a home. Saw-tooth cuts and curves shaped crest with an incised leaf pattern. Reeding on uprights; paneled; top of baseboard is nicely rounded and grooved. As is now: 77"l x 31½"h x 57"w. $475.00.

BED
Oak and poplar woods; the half roll at top is 6"dia. Applied factory carvings decorate crest, fluted and leaf finials' curls, and baseboard. Has the air of the nineteenth century. Top 84"h x 59"w. Baseboard 39"h. $895.00.

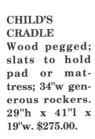

CHILD'S CRADLE
Wood pegged; slats to hold pad or mattress; 34"w generous rockers. 29"h x 41"l x 19"w. $275.00.

ENGLISH OAK ARMOIRE

Carried to the States many years ago. Carvings, incisings, beading below high pediment; embellishments with burl outlining drawers; beautiful brass pulls in two styles; beveled glass in side doors; inside shelves. Unusually fine. 88"h x 79"w x 21½"dp. $6,500.00.

ARMOIRE

Homes that could afford armoires didn't have to use hooks hung openly about a room for holding garments. These pre-dated the standard built-in wardrobes. Plain and quarter-cut with a darker stained applied center crest, brief door trims, and hardware; interesting panel treatment, a wide base drawer, and an inside tie or belt rack. 76"h x 48"w x 20"dp. $275.00.

ARMOIRE

This four-door flat-back piece was a storage unit for choir robes in a nineteenth century church; brass fixtures with a top shelf in each compartment. These were movable or attached to a wall, sometimes they were built-in. Called armoires in France, here in America they were often known as clothes-closets and clothes-cupboards. 84"h x 57"w x 14"dp. $1,800.00.

ARMOIRE

Note placement of the plain and quarter-sawn panels — its only attempt at decoration; self wood knobs on the drawer, a brass door knob on a blackened iron keeper. 78'h x 36'w x 17'dp. $400.00.

Benches and Stools

KNEELING STOOL
(Prayer Stool, Prie Dieux)
Dark-stained oak; mass produced
in the late 1800s. A rest for the
elbows; and a bench for the knees.
26"h x 18"w x 16½"dp. $155.00.

STOOL
Heavy twisted wire base holding a double
wood seat with a small crack in the top
layer. 24"h. Seat 12"dia. $95.00.

LADDER STEPSTOOL/CHAIR

Oak, birdseye maple, walnut; iron and brass fixtures; wood pegged; opens into four steps. 37"h. Seat 16"w x 16¼"dp. $58.00.

PIANO/ORGAN STOOL
Oak and birch woods; age and usage have worn and split the original black leather on the revolving seat. Ca. 1870; base is unusually handsome, factory incisings and tiny animal paw feet. 20½"h. Seat 14"dia. $300.00 as is.

ORGAN STOOL
Original red, green, and gold floral upholstery framed in oak; walnut turned base post; three iron legs have been recently gilded. 20"h. Seat 12"square. $125.00.

PIANO BENCH
Underside label printed: "Standard Piano Bench Co." Chicago. Built-in adjustment for various heights. Piano and organ stools have become popular extras as chairs while the flat-top benches can be plant-stands or chairside tables. Ref.; 20½" x 25"w x 14¼"dp. $145.00.

SHAKER STOOL
Oak with pine; wood pegged; splayed legs. Quakers believed in a simple unity of well proportioned parts in making their furniture, practicality always foremost. 19"h x 19½"w x 11"dp. $85.00.

STOOL
Heavy; oak and mixed woods; wire-firmed slightly splayed legs; seat depressed in center.; Note careful construction; finial base center. 22"h. Seat 15"dia. $125.00.

SHOE SHINE STAND
Thinly upholstered oak seat supported by iron wire and bands. Wood covered footrest; original bright mustard yellow paint has in hard usage become faded until only traces remain. 36"l. Seat 14"h x 10"dia. $135.00.

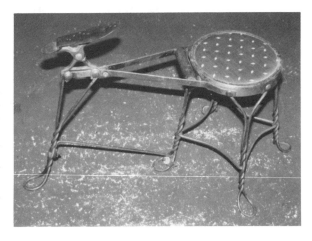

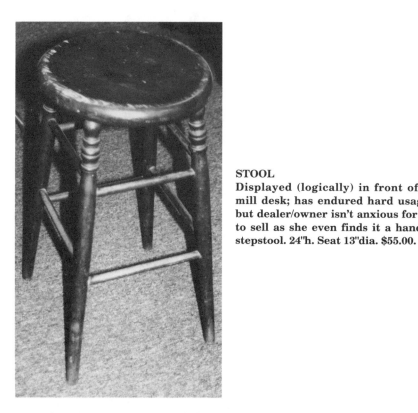

STOOL
Displayed (logically) in front of a mill desk; has endured hard usage but dealer/owner isn't anxious for it to sell as she even finds it a handy stepstool. 24"h. Seat 13"dia. $55.00.

UTILITY BENCH
Type much used for a laundry tub bench; stained dark, with heavy construction. 36½"l x 17½"h x 18"dp. $28.00.

Bookcases and Desks

S ROLL DESK
Dated 1886; parallel thin wood slats, fastened to a flexible backing, can be lifted up by the finger slots in the wood handles and slid smoothly up under the ledge, this exposing the desk space and many nooks and cubicles for desk accessories; has pullout shelf on one side; plain grain and quartered. 44"h x 43"w x 30"dp. $1,995.00.

PLANTATION DESK
Golden oak; personnel and operation records were kept in the drawers and slots inside the spaces uncovered by the dropfront. The two small drawers below the long one are uncommon; brass knobs and pulls; thin columns appear at each side of the tall gallery, their finials above that uncommonly placed shelf; fluting and a center-crest carving combined with molding. Note the fancifully designed legs and the reeding above. 64"h x 40"w x 22"dp. $1,375.00.

SECRETARY-DESK

Typifying their European influence, American manufacturers made custom-built furniture, adding a few of their own ideas. This elegant combination piece has a hinged dropfront covering a work surface and pigeonholes with a small door cubicle; elaborate embellishments of applied carvings, incisings, turnings, columns, burl inlays, and the like. 69"h x 32"w x 16½"dp. $895.00.

CHILD'S ROLLTOP DESK
Needs refinishing. Incisings; drawers all dovetailed; side-paneled and cutback sides under the writing ledge; brass Victorian style pulls; dark stained oak. 42½"h x 30½"w x 19½"dp. $395.00 as is.

BOOKCASE/DESK
Ca. first quarter 1900s. Two deep open shelves; dropfront writing surface; brass knobs on the two black stained additional units inside; arched gallery with applied factory machined pediment. 43½"h x 32"w x 18"dp. $375.00.

SCHOOL DESK

Uncommonly fine even though it shows lots of children's usage. Iron fixtures (topside bands may have been added sometime during the years for strengthening); iron bolts further aid sturdiness; note the large dovetails on the outside; on top are a 1½" pen/pencil groove and an inkwell hole; inside the desk is another ½"dp x 2"w groove for miscellaneous supplies, the long groove stretching the width of the desk; lift top slanted toward the 8"w seat is made for more comfortable writing or reading surface; each side of the cast iron base is prominently embossed: "EDUCATIONAL" on one side and "B'HAM" (meaning Birmingham) on the other side. Some child has carved a big initial "H" into the seat. 32"h. $175.00.

FOLDUP SEAT SCHOOL DESK
Cast iron with oak; factories have turned out thousands of these styles. On top is a short pencil groove and the customary hole for an ink bottle; under the slanted lift top is ample space for supplies. The folding seat at front is for the child ahead whose desk also has a seat in front for the next child ahead, and so on up the aisle. 26½"h x 21"w. $45.00.

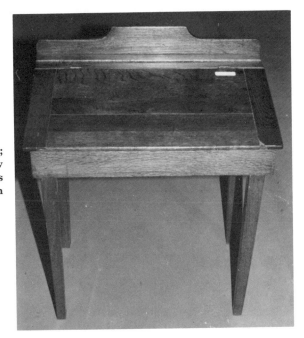

CHILD'S DESK
Forward-slant lift top; pencil groove, low gallery and brass hinges. 23"h bk x 19"h frt x 13"dp. $45.00.

CHILD'S KNEEHOLE DESK
While I was taking photos at a Fernandina Beach, Florida, mall, one of the dealers excitedly asked me to go out and see a desk she'd just found on a trip northeast — still in her van (so that's where the picture was taken). All original; nailed mortised drawers; center writing space is black canvas (uncommon); stamped on the back is this label: "PARIS MFG. CO., South Paris, Maine"; (they were famous cabinetmakers). It's a treasure. 34"h x 26¾"w x 18"dp. $475.00.

DROP FRONT BOOKCASE/DESK
Pale golden oak; mission style; original keys available for glass doors and front. Opens to reveal shelves and vertical cubicles; narrow metal rods control dropfront writing surface — felt covered. 57"h x 30½"w x 14½"dp. $635.00.

STACK BOOKCASE
Popular beyond the turn of the century — and now still greatly in demand; made in individual sections so they could be low or high according to personal preferences, space, and needs; each glass framed front could be lifted out and up, to slide back on top rails. The top cornice in itself can be lifted off and used as a book rack — or whatever. Brass knobs; stamped by maker: "HALE'S BOOK-CASE, HERKIMER, NEW YORK." 63"h x 48"w x 9½"dp. $650.00.

BOOKCASE
Refinished to the original in a pale golden oak; five shelves; wood casters; a wide cornice with edge-applied moldings. At each of the front corners is a deeply carved lion's head with an open mouth — roaring (rare on such furniture). Now used as a china cabinet. 69"h x 43½"w x 12"dp. $1,145.00.

BOOKCASE
Two doors and four shelves; random width boards form the back; pediment of scrolled leaves on reed-edge shelf with top of solid sides; nickel on iron keykeeper — key gone; tiny apron. 64"h x 45½"w x 3"dp. $1,095.00.

BOOKCASE
Two doors with brass pull and escutcheon; top shelf is reeded; bracket sides; apron forms into front feet. 57½"h x 36½"w x 12½"dp. $745.00.

BOOKCASE
Two doors, each with its original key; brass fixtures; wide overhang top. These are today more extensively bought for use as china cabinets. 60"h x 48"w x 14"dp. $875.00.

BOOKCASE
Handsomely grained pale golden oak; two doors; brass fixtures; adjustable shelves; tiny gallery and apron. 58"h x 36"w x 12½"dp. $745.00.

REVOLVING BOOK RACK
Dated October 17, 1893, Chicago, Illinois; book storage in lower shelf; a tilted place to lean a book with a strip at bottom to prevent slippage; an inverted ball finial joins at center with the three office type legs; iron rod and holding screw. 45"h x 15"sq. $375.00.

STORE DESK
Counter top; lift top as a hinged sloping lid under which is generous storage space and pigeonholes. The one large pullout drawer is dovetailed, while its pull is incised squared brass; grooved base all around. 6"h x 29½"w x 19½"dp. $125.00.

BOOKCASE/DESK, SIDE by SIDE, or COMBINATION BOOKCASE and DESK
Homemakers (especially in rural districts) cherished these "parlor pieces" from the late 1800s into the early 1900s...and now they have again surfaced in demand. Pressed and applied carvings with a dot-and-dash pattern outline one side of the cabinet with its adjustable shelves; much attention to detail — even flower patterns on the brass pulls, escutcheons, and knobs; note the feet; elaborate gallery; dropfront writing surface fronts many cubicles. Besides books, the shelves are ideal for displaying (and keeping from the reach of small children) precious bric-a-brac. 71"h x 48½"w x 16"dp. $1,695.00.

SIDE by SIDE
Unusual shaping of the thick beveled mirror; heavily incised and machine carvings; uncommon gallery; a kerosene or coal oil lamp placed on the middle shelf illuminated the writing surface provided by the dropfront; compartments inside the desk; bowfront door and drawers; brass fixtures, and claw feet. In the late 1890s, the Sears catalog showed a similar furniture item with a special price of $11.00, which could also be ordered in imitation mahogany for $11.50. 74"h x 36"w x 13"dp. $1,495.00.

SIDE by SIDE
Exceptionally fine combination piece; rarely seen concave curved drawer above the dropfront desk compartment; note the brass drawer openers; the knobs on the swell front and flat wide drawers are plain, while the door knob and those on the top concave front drawer are designed; fine quality cornice; reeding, fluting, slim turned columns; two beveled mirrors were removed for replacement, the larger back-stamped: "DEC. 1899;" there was more but too worn off to be deciphered; found in West Virginia. 72"h x 44"w x 20"dp. $1,345.00.

BOOKCASE/WRITING DESK
or SECRETARY

Very popular but cost a bit more than most furniture. In 1897 Sears advertised it as solid oak, some with quarter-sawn units, others made entirely from birch; as then, this has adjustable shelves; thick beveled glass mirror with "fancy" molding; brass hardware; machine carved trims; the dropfront desk space interior has pigeonhole compartments. 67"h x 41"w x 14"dp. $800.00.

SIDE by SIDE

Ca. 1895; golden oak; dampness in storage has discolored mirror which can easily be restored as described on page 128; bowfront door; brass fixtures; applied carvings and molding on arched crest; bracket sides legs; rounded shelves. 74"h x 42"w x 16"dp. $795.00.

Cabinets and Cupboards

CHINA CABINET
All original with swell-front glass doors and shelves; small paw feet; brass key survives. Ea. side is 17½" curved. Overall 62½"h x 36" across the back. $1,295.00.

CHINA CABINET
All original; has the key; bowed-out front and sides; quarter-sawn wood; five swell-front shelves and curved-back gallery; large lions' claws on wooden balls — this combination very difficult now to find in that mostly one sees the glass balls. 68"h x 40"w x 16"dp. $1,295.00.

CHINA CABINET
Mission style; moderately bowfront; original glass, no keys, and side frame posts continue to form the feet; top crosspiece forms a low gallery. 54"h x 36"w x 13"dp. $485.00.

"SHOW" and "STORE" CABINET/CUPBOARD
Black iron hardware; sliding and knob latch pulls; groovings, and an unusual roll-center winged cornice with applied carvings. 72"h x 36"w x 16"dp. $850.00.

KITCHEN CUPBOARD

Collapsible — uncommon cabinet; top lifts off, shelves lift out, top doors come off, side hinges fold flat — for transporting — or for using the lower part as a chest if desired — or in a limited space of a room; iron turn latches hold firm upper and lower doors and other fixtures are brass knobs and iron hinges; three inside top shelves — one lower; one long drawer; key keeper — no remaining key; a very interesting cupboard in two separate usable sections. 72"h x 30"w x 16"dp. $695.00

KITCHEN CUPBOARD

Ca. 1910; refinished to nut-brown from original white; paint traces stubbornly adhere to pores on inside shelves (note the top one is cut farther out for the door catches;) pores do seem to defy paint removers after absorbing the casein-based colors of long ago; stepback worksheck is 2"w; both sides at top, bottom, and center have 3"dia screened ventilation holes; brass hardware. 74"h x 38"w x 24"dp. $895.00.

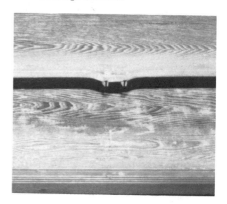

KITCHEN CUPBOARD
Factory dovetailing (the round scallops) on four corners of both drawers having designed brass replacement pulls; in some areas cupboards as these — with its big round screen-covered hole low on each side for ventilation — were called pie safes; wide raised edge cornice forms a slipoff protector for articles placed on the top outside shelf. 71"h x 36"w x 15"dp. $685.00.

KITCHEN CABINET
(THE ENGLISH HOOSIER)

Fine grained English oak; many labels inside doors; one: The Minor Model Easiwork Kitchen Cabinet; on another: three weeks' menus printed on paper lists; middle doors have instructions for: "Care of the Cabinet and First Aid in the Home;" there is a spice rack, a cookbook holder, and near the top of the right side is a nickel-plated iron towel (or apron) hook; with matching door and drawer fixtures and hinges; a white enamel work shelf over a wooden pull-out dough-rolling ledge; white painted flour container/sifter; the interior of the right bottom drawer is tin-lined while the top drawer has three divided compartments. Differing from the American Hoosier Cabinet: the English has solid rather than glass doors, and a black-edged white porcelain enamel work shelf. 72"h x 30½"w x 17½"dp. $495.00.

"HOOSIER" KITCHEN CABINET

Ca. 1910; long door hides a flour container with a glass pane on two swingout bars, glass sugar container can also be swung out; frosted and etched patterned glass doors have shelves behind them; the base door hides a wire rack; vitreous enamel work shelf; a wooden rollup curtain comes down over the shelf (with the glass jars on it). 89"h x 39½"w x 27½"dp. $1,495.00.

KITCHEN CABINET/CUPBOARD
Brass and blackened iron fixtures; pullout drawer under white enamel work shelf; short drawer above alcove area which has a wood slat pulldown door; casters. "Hoosier" style. 70"h x 48"w x 27½"dp. $995.00.

PIE SAFE
Hard to find size — no longer easily found in the marketplaces. Many were made from poplar. Homemade; screen used instead of customary pierced tins inside the door frames; dull brass knob and hinges with a whittled turn strip (seen so often on very old pieces) at top center to keep doors closed; overhang top makes a wide shelf; the four frame sides continue into legs; three deep inside shelves; the safe is a 19" to 20" height, enough to accommodate jugs, crocks, firkins, and such, whatever was desired to be stored under there; a mouse once nibbled the center corner of one door — and rather than being a detriment, to most buyers, this is generally considered a plus. 39"h x 29"w x 16"dp. $475.00.

PIE SAFE

Primitively hand built; new screening nailed on — may have had to replace original damaged pierced tins; new white china knobs; original whittled wood turn holds top and bottom; one-board sides; wide front boards end in bracket feet; pie safes, especially those that fit nicely into modern homes, are increasingly difficult to find. 60"h x 38"w x 20½"dp. $595.00.

CABINET/CHEST

Pine bottom glass knob drawers; brass hinged top; chamfered edges; two-board sides. 37"h x 19"w x 19"dp. $125.00.

SMALL CUPBOARD
Ca. 1840; dark stained oak; stepback shelf; inside shelves in top and base sections; quality cornice; hinges need restoring; brass fixtures; each side is one-board 12½"w ending in bracket feet. 36"h x 22"w x 14"dp. $1,350.00.

LOW CABINET
Black stained oak; brass hinges, slide-pulls on the doors were (enthusiastically) painted white along with the two inside shelves, and lingering in the fluted gallery; each side panel is deeply incised in a crisscross design — it too with traces of paint; an appealing small piece still sturdy and able to give long-time usefulness if properly refinished to an owner's wishes. 35½"h x 26"w x 14"dp. $150.00.

CABINET
Handmade in western Kentucky a generation or two ago; designed with imagination for a white veined marble top, one drawer with self knobs, a handy shelf, fluting, and curves; whorl feet. 30"h x 24"w x 14"dp. $275.00.

MUSIC CABINET
Seen in north Georgia; quarter-cut modified swell front door with brass pull and hinges, opening to reveal six shelves amply sized to hold sheet music, etc.; beveled glass not quite perfect after being stored away; slightly curved legs with claw feet at front and plain tapering at back. 40"h x 19"w. $365.00.

WALL HANGING CORNER CUPBOARD

Ca. 1780; English oak resembling dark American walnut; paneled trim door; grooved cornice (cornices of this general style represent skilled cabinetmakers); all brass fixtures — the large "H" hinges, and a tiny brass knob with an elaborate escutcheon whose remaining original key opens the door to three faded blue/green painted "Cupid's bow" edged shelves. 46"h. Ea side 22" slanted to corner. $775.00.

MEDICINE CABINET

Complements a dressing room today; unusually fine cabinetmaking with overall square lines; drawer front has a deeper stained pattern with ivory inlays; that drawer and the door have brass teardrop pulls; brass hinges; reedings and applied moldings with a mushroom finial at the center of a broken pediment — this not often seen, along with the inlay, on such pieces; inside shelves. 23"h x 15"w x 11"dp. $375.00.

SEWING CABINET
Made from English oak; brass chains to control the top's lift, brass hinges and "posey knob"; deep top receptacle and narrow drawer are red satin lined; plain grain and quartered; wood casters; and a shelf underneath all. 22"h x 20½"w x 13¾"dp. $145.00.

SPOOL CABINET
Once used by a village dressmaker; top lifts open; top section with access only from the lid; key missing; two drawers are dovetailed and have removable sections making separate spaces to store spools of several sizes; brass fixtures. 21"h x 13¼"w x 11"dp. $375.00.

SPOOL CABINET
Unusual; three bentwood oak pieces form top and sides; veneered front; very heavy flat base; flower lines are etched and darkened on drawer fronts whose pulls are uncommon solid brass pendulum types; on the cabinet's back is a deeply grooved flower pattern with "Xs"and a "50" in three places — a double circle with "50" in three arcs on the outside ring. 24"h x 16"across. $795.00.

SPOOL CABINET
Used today as a low chairside table; the eight slim brass handles open drawers with mortised corners; in black is stamped: "J. & P. COATS BEST SIX CORD SPOOL COTTON"; on the cabinet's back is labeled in a gold and black circle: "J. & P. COATS BEST SIX CORD" and at center is "50." 15"h x 20½"w x 15½"dp. $750.00.

FILE CABINET
Ca. 1910; three stacks, top has one drawer, each of the other two stacks has two drawers; brass fixtures — rods slide in for wooden dividers; heavy pulls; slip-in frames for drawer labels; sturdy base frame and squared feet. 51"h x 17"w x 26½"dp. $435.00.

STORE CABINET

Ca. late 1800s into 1900s; (could have been part of a longer counter in a big store or used alone in a country general store;) wooden pulls on drawers; brass knob on door; black iron slide-latch may be new; brass bound keyhole keepers; plain and quarter-sawn oak; the top two drawers overhang. 42"h x 54"w x 19"dp. $550.00.

DRILL BIT CABINET

Sitting on store cabinet; ca. early 1900s; quarter-cut and plain grain; original black iron doorlatch; brass pulls; behind the cabinet door are a number of boxes; a dropfront cover gives access to 18 little partitions. 27"h x 26"w x 11½"dp. $575.00.

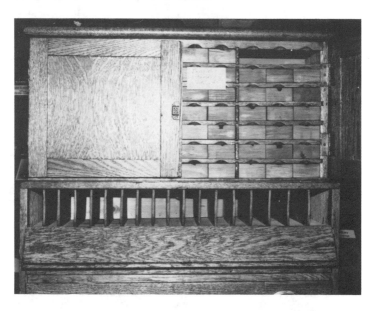

COUNTRY STORE DESK

On a primitive homemade base; black leather in good condition centers the chamfered edge lift top; each of the six drawers has small dovetailed corners and large hollow brass pull-knobs; top ledge has a cutout groove for writing tools and a hole for an ink bottle. Inside that top space was a rolled-up picture one often finds in old trunks and such, from the early 1900s, of family reunions, church picnics, town celebrations, and so on; note the wide-brimmed hats on the men and their ties on what was probably a warm day — and the hats on the children. (Thought you might enjoy seeing it — I did). Desk 15"h x 39"w x 24"dp. $525.00.

STORE CABINET

Narrow 1" pullout shelf at the reeded base with tiny brass knob; large brass pulls for dovetailed drawers; low gallery; brass bound hole for the inkwell space. 18"h x 40"w x 22"dp. $395.00.

Chairs

ARMCHAIR
Ca. 1915; upholstering is not usual on this rustic furniture; all original eye caning, and carvings resembling vines on tree bark. After the Civil War, this rustic treatment became very popular, seen in cast iron pieces, and usually one-of-a-kind in oak, as seen here — also in hickory; these continued into the early 1900s. 32"h x 23" x 26" overall width. Seat 15"fl. $400.00.

ARMCHAIR
Ca. 1860 – 80; Elizabethan Revival. When Jenny Lind, the "Swedish Nightingale," made her triumphal American tour sponsored by P.T. Barnum, two of Philadelphia's skilled cabinetmakers presented her with a low Gothic substyle bed having innumerable bobbin-and-ball turnings. All such beds then became "Jenny Linds," and the name universally spread to other heavily spooled furniture pieces. Though Elizabethan styles are loosely grouped with spool turnings, their turnings are larger (fine spool turnings achieved by factory specialists). Here a thin pierced wood seat may have replaced an original one caned or upholstered; the scrolled headpiece tops a gracefully outcurved splat — its plainness perfect with such a profusion of spools. 37"h. Seat 10"w frt x 18"dp x 16"fl. $225.00.

 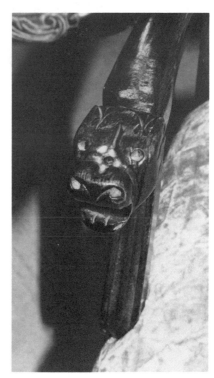

FORMAL ARMCHAIR
Original green crushed velvet upholstery; elaborate crest with a center face; each armrest ends in a lion's head with open mouth and laid back ears; light eyes and nostrils; deep incisings. 44"h x 23½"w. Seat 19"dp x 17"fl. $575.00.

55

ARMCHAIR
Ca. 1920s; white seat cover restored; one arm quarter-cut, one arm plain grain; turned-under ends of arm rests attributed to "Pennsylvania Knuckles"; barley twists, reeding, and banisters. 40"h. Seat 22"w frt x 17"w bk x 18"dp x 17"fl. $165.00.

ARMCHAIR
Ca. 1920; mission oak style; restored watered-silk upholstery in seat; cutout center on headpiece lightens overall straight lines. 38"h. Seat 20½"w x 19"dp x 17"fl. $188.00.

ROCKING CHAIR
Victorian; restored seat and headpiece upholstering; dark stained oak and elm; two short wide balusters with bell-shaped cutouts; deeply pressed designs. 39"h. Seat 18½"w x 18"dp x 15½"fl. $145.00.

ARMCHAIR
Small armrests; long turned spindles, legs and front stretchers; deep saddle seat; top and center slats "Boston" types. 42"h. Seat 17"dp x 16"fl. $125.00.

ARMCHAIR
Barrel style; all original black leather upholstery which is tufted on sides and back; wood frame 2½" thick; each side is one piece of solid oak from floor to top sides; deeply comfortable. 38"h x 23"dp x 8"fl. $225.00.

ARMCHAIR
Embossed paper seat; plain and quarter-cut; bentwood arms; one low turned stretcher in front; extra-wide and narrow back crosspieces, ball finials. 37½"h. Seat 21"w frt x 16"bk x 19"dp x 17"fl. $143.00.

ARMCHAIR
Factory produced in the late 1800s; original black leather restored with brasshead pins; graceful legs end in split-toed animal feet; sometimes known as office or desk furniture. 40"h x 22"w x 20"dp x 16"fl. $165.00.

INVALID'S CHAIR
Ca. 1850; combined woods; dealers might call it a "French style"; liftup lid; iron hardware. 33"h. Seat 24"w x 19"dp x 16"fl. $360.00.

ARMCHAIR
Purchased by a collector when a Lake Ontario yacht club redecorated its dining room; the club had at an earlier date replaced the black leather back and seat, using big brass head nails; mint condition after a lot of mileage. 34½"h. Seat 20¼"w x 18"dp x 17¾"fl. $125.00.

OFFICE CHAIR
Swivel seat; floral and butterflies pattern on pressed paper seat fastened with brass head nails — probably not the original but old; five turned back spindles and four plain ones with one metal spindle under each arm; shallow pressed design in headrest. 42"h. Seat 20½"w x 18½"dp. $275.00.

JUDGE'S COURTROOM CHAIR
Leather with iron fixtures; swivels and tilts back; wood stick and ball designs; casters. No price. If ever available, a similar might be valued $275.00 – 325.00.

DESK CHAIR
Ca. 1890 – 1900. Swivel seat; restored thin red velvet on seat; iron rollers and iron base center; softly curved arms on this heavy chair displaying that attention to detail spared what could have been severity of form. 40"h. Seat 20"w x 18½"dp x 18"fl. $165.00.

OFFICE CHAIR
Three-way adjustable; patent dated April 23, 1895; wood, iron, leather shoulder rest. 36½"h. Seat 17"dia. $135.00.

SCHOOLROOM CHAIR
Four slats form underseat shelf for school supplies; this slat construction is uncommon and adds to value. If the piece had a left-hand writing surface it would be even more uncommon. Arm is 9"w x 36"h. Seat 18"w x 15½"dp x 18"fl. $85.00.

YOUTH CHAIR

Bentwood in four continuing single piece sections; restored eye caning; underseat is signed: "Michael Thonet, Inverted Bentwood Chair 1840, Vienna, Austria"; wood pegged; footrest is pinned at all four uprights. 34"h. Seat 15"dia bk x 12"dia. $195.00.

RECLINER (MORRIS STYLE)

Ca. 1900; loose cushions replaced; oak and iron construction; rod used to adjust angle of chair back (this an adaptation of early Egyptian methods); tongue and grooved wood seat. William Morris, the English craftsman, being of ample girth, found Victorian chairs uncomfortable. About 1865 he evolved this idea of a more commodious type. His concepts were activated in American factories until about 1915, by manufacturers such as Charles P. Limbert Co. at Grand Rapids, Michigan, Elbert Hubbard of Aurora, New York, and the Stickley family factories at Grand Rapids, Michigan and Eastwood, New York; all were primarily interested in functionalism according to the tenets of the Arts and Crafts Movement. 38½"h x 29½"w x 33½"dp. $225.00.

PLATFORM ROCKER
Also known as "Spring Rocker"; ca. 1880s; combined oak and maple stripped to the natural woods and wax-finished, with darkened rings to resemble bamboo; Eastlake favored this style; it wouldn't rock about and wear out the carpeting; iron springs; back and seat covered with carpet strips. 39"h. Seat 15"w x 16"dp x 13½"fl. $235.00.

PLATFORM ROCKER
Ca. 1880s; patterned velvet upholstery; iron hardware, springs, and
fixture to keep chair from tipping
far back; wide pressed pattern top
slat with two narrower ones below;
nine turned spindles in back with
five under arms; arm-to-back side
braces; finials. 42"h. Seat 21"w x
17½"dp x 14"fl. $275.00.

RECLINER

Morris style/mission. Ca. 1890; this differs from usual mission furniture in that it has the wood-framed pullout footrest, which can be folded back flat and nested in the wire basket; restored cushions, backrest cushion tufted to provide head support; generous arms, lightly curved front legs with claw feet; factory made. 39"h. Seat 21"sq x 15"fl. $500.00.

THEATER SEATS
Slatted as commonly used for summer stock theaters. In sets of two.
Stamped in black ink on back of each seat is: "Elastic Chair Co.,
Titusville, Penn."; iron fixtures; feathered wings and swirls designs
pressed on the top rail and lower back slat — rarely seen; two joined
at the floor; two sets available. 34"h x 62"w x 17"dp. $175.00 total.

THEATER SEATS (MOVIE HOUSE STYLE) Patent dates from the 1920s to 1931; oak veneer steamed into comfortable backs and seats; iron reinforced corners; lift seats. 33½"h x 36½"w x 15½"fl. $55.00 set.

THEATER SEATS Three oak veneer sections; curved seats fold flat against concave backs; wood armrests with rounded fronts; metal sides partially decorated with applied brass lines, roundels, rectilinear columns; iron frames. 34"h x 61"w x 16½"dp. $50.00 set.

WHEELCHAIR
Footrest; iron, wire, and rubber
tires; saddle seat; a small wheel at
the back to aid steering; comfortable rolled and curved armrest.
39"h x 20½"w x 18"fl. $250.00.

WHEELCHAIR
Two front wheels and two at the
back are wood and wire with rubber rims. Seen in a far northwest
corner of New York State at a huge
exposition. 53"h. Seat 19"w x 19½"dp.
$100.00 as is. Restored with caning
as shown on original leg protector,
$250.00.

WHEELCHAIR
Fold-up footrests; brass fasteners; iron wire spokes on rubber covered iron wheels. Seen in a big barn shop in rural north central Georgia. 48"h x 23½"w. $95.00.

ROCKING CHAIR
THE "LITTLE BOSTON"
Ca. 1850; the typical Windsor headpiece became standardized after 1835. This could have been used as a nursing chair (so baby could be fed or rocked without bumping it against side arms), a sewing rocker, or even to sit upon while stringing beans or shelling peas, to be close to the pans on the floor; turned "knees" below the seat; rockers are socketed into the legs — rear legs widely splayed; five spindles; side stretchers are so low, this might have started out as a straight chair. 31"h. Seat 18"w x 19"dp x 16"fl. $225.00.

SLIPPER ROCKING CHAIR

Also regionally called Nursing or Sewing Rocker; pressed headpiece with the same pattern on two slats; eight stick and spool turned spindles; pressed paper replaced the original seat; mushroom finials; wood was dark stained. Putting on ladies' footwear — slippers that were laced around the ankles and insteps with ribbons, or high shoes that had to be buttoned up — was a lot easier with these low chairs. 39"h. Seat 17"w frt x 16"dp x 16"fl. $195.00.

ROCKING CHAIR

Spindles are white oak; slimness of the seven center spindles indicates an earlier date than those more thickly made; rest of the chair is mixed woods; factories only made these rockers for special orders because they were considered "country chairs" and strictly for comfort with no place in formal rooms; replacement seat an effort to look like the original; uncommon wide brass bands wrap around the uprights. 45"h x 19"w. Seat 7½"dp. $235.00.

ROCKING CHAIR
Ca. 1870 – 80. Thoughtfully designed in golden oak; applied carvings; ball, barley twist, and button spindles with larger spiral twists on uprights; serpentine curved slats; side braces, and a curved apron; plain and quarter-cut. 37½"h. Seat 16"w x 17½"fl. $245.00.

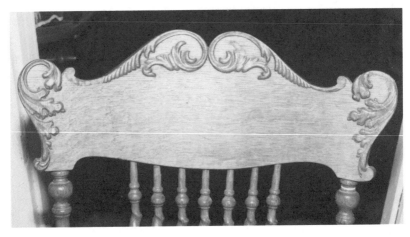

ARROWBACK ROCKING CHAIR
Golden oak; shallow-pressed crest; flattened arrow spindles; reupholstered. 36"h. Seat 17"w frt x 15½"w bk x 16½"fl. $175.00.

ROCKING CHAIR
Fanback spool-turned spindles; curved headpiece with applied edge carvings; depressed center saddle-curved seat; only the two front stretchers are stick and button turned; very tall; thick stiles taper at the crest. 34"h. Seat 20"w frt x 18"dp x 16"fl. $225.00.

ROCKING CHAIR
Pressed paper replacement seat over space originally caned; deeply pressed flower pattern on curved headpiece and two narrow slats; small side braces. 40½"h. Seat 20"w frt x 18"w bk x 16½"fl. $225.00.

ROCKING CHAIR
Golden oak; deep saddle seat; pressed headpiece; after 1800 rocking chairs generally had curved armrests; these typically factory made. 40"h. Seat 19¾"w x 20"dp x 17"fl. $175.00.

ROCKING CHAIR
Preponderance of end spools and button turnings, along with extra-pretty finials, are the only decorations on this curve-crested rocker with its knuckle-finger armrests, the whole very attractive — and looks comfortable. 41"h. Seat 20½"w x 19"dp x 15"fl. $145.00.

ROCKING CHAIR
Ca. 1840; arrowback with headpiece and two other slats fastened to long sideposts topped with "donkey" or "rabbit" ears, achieved by flattening the top front sides; typical style of the 1830s and 1840s in New York State and western New England. When stretchers are so low, rockers may have been added to an originally straight chair — here the legs are socketed on; bowed-out armrests; splayed legs; seat is oak and rest of chair is maple. 41"h x 16"w x 17"dp. $295.00.

YOUTH ROCKING CHAIR
Ca. 1910; jigsaw cutouts on a wide flowerpot splat and at the finger-hold on the imaginatively decorated wide headpiece; incisings; many pierced holes with a star center of smaller holes in the round wood seat insert held by brasshead tacks; legs are fastened into the rockers; typically Victorian easing over into the early 1900s. 34½"h. Seat 21"w frt x 15"w bk x 16"fl. $235.00.

ROCKING CHAIR
Golden oak; pressed design on crest and tops of stiles; sides continuing from the headpiece forming the arms and curving onto the seat are considered Pennsylvania design; saddle seat; under arm iron rods added to spindles. 45"h. Seat 19"w x 17½"dp x 16"fl. $185.00.

ROCKING CHAIR
Fanned uprights typical of "country" rockers; saddle seat; side braces; pressed headpiece with roundel center; acorn and button finials. 32"h. Seat 16½"w x 16"dp x 16"fl. $125.00.

PRIMITIVE ROCKER
Ca. 1890; inexpensively made in a backyard project; comfortable and easy to carry; canvas back can be slipped off wood uprights for folding the chair or washing the cover; canvas strip arms; dowel rod type stretchers. 33"h. Seat 22"w frt. $18.00.

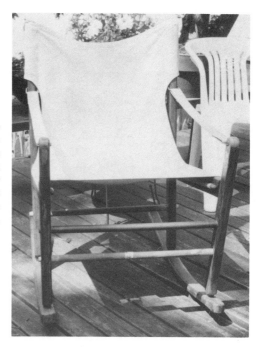

BANISTER BACK ROCKER
Ca. 1910; all original with leather seat; factory made and ample enough for anyone. 39½"h x 24"w x 20½"dp. $125.00.

ROCKING CHAIR
Oak and elm; pressed back; saddle seat; many turnings on the six spindles, posts under armrests, legs, stiles, and stretcher. 39"h. Seat 18½"w x 18"dp x 15½"fl. $175.00.

ROCKING CHAIR
Plain and quarter-cut. Ca. 1890 –
1900; reupholstered; banister
back and conventional crest.
41½"h x 23½"w x 20"dp. $125.00.

ROCKING CHAIR
Buttons and balls among the turnings; seven spindles with wide
pressed headpiece; much mileage
on worn saddle seat which is bowed
down; factory produced during the
last quarter of the 1800s. 35"h. Seat
18¼"w x 17½"dp x 14½"fl. $185.00.

80

ROCKING CHAIR

Nut-brown oak stain; seat and crest reupholstered, matched closely to shreds of the original fabric; iron springs inside seat; no stretchers; barley twists and flat button turnings on spindles, with larger spirals on the stiles; finials look like beehives; scalloped apron. 40"h (to top of finials). Seat 19"w x 17"dp x 16"fl. $225.00.

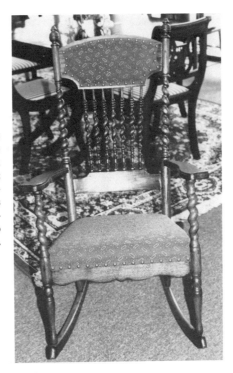

ROCKING CHAIR

Found at a Pennsylvania estate auction of nineteenth century furniture; new eye caning; ornately pressed and carved; note the center reeding of the upright "rolls"; the narrow seat apron is cut out at each side to allow room for the large ball knees; crest design is repeated on the two lower slats. 41"h. Seat 20½"w x 19"dp x 15"fl. $275.00.

ROCKING CHAIR

While the pressed paper seat is not the original, it is an old one — with center eagle holding a snake in its claws and other designs circling it; three spindles and matching post arms are reinforced by iron rods; vase shaped splat and pressed headpiece above ball-and-spool turned stiles; all four legs not customarily designed with turnings that match the posts, the two front legs splayed; note all are set into the rockers. Seat center is 12"dia. 35"h. Seat 18"w frt x 17"w bk x 18"dp x 15"fl. $285.00.

ROCKING CHAIR

A rarity; bentwood caned loop back where one bentwood strip continues from the seat on one side, up over the back, and down to form the armrest on the other; arch supported under-seat stretches from one edge-cut leg to the other; two legs at back are plain, squared and splayed; a short fretwork splat has three pattern turned spindles on each side; overall the parts of this unusual rocker seem to flow gracefully into their joinings with others. 42"h. Seat 21"w x 18"dp. $325.00.

ROCKING CHAIR

Ca. 1910; a heavy, vastly comfortable chair with "different" lines; seat and back reupholstered; note the animal feet fastened onto the top of the rockers; note also the shaping of the sides joining with the posts, and the corner indentations of the headpiece; short back rockers. 34"h. Seat 21"w x 20"dp x 16"fl. $185.00.

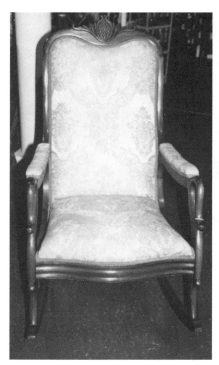

ROCKING CHAIR
Brocade, gimp edged, restored closely as possible to the original pattern; swan-carved arm fronts continue halfway down the legs; applied pineapple crest (the early colonial symbol of hospitality); fluted seat apron. 41"h x 25"w. Seat 21"dp. $325.00.

REFINISHED CHILD'S ROCKER
A rare piece; from the Victorians; cut velvet seat restored to original; golden and deeper stains; the whole chair is elaborately made with curved arms; plain side spindles; seven at back with button and ball turnings; spool knees below curve-front seat; an unusually wide crest deeply pressed with dragon heads, wings, a fountain urn of flowers, and more. 31½"h. Seat 17½"w x 17"dp x 13"fl. $285.00.

CHILD'S ROCKING CHAIR
Restored rolled seat of plywood; quarter-cut and plain grain; deeply pressed crest pattern in a grooved and beading frame; wide splat. 30"h x 13½"w x 18"dp x 10"fl. $135.00.

CHILD'S VICTORIAN ROCKER
Ca. 1860; inlaid with lighter maple; shield type splat has a burl inlaid center; turnings and incisings; note the termination of the arms in a small dropoff knuckle roll at each side. 24"h. Seat 11"w bk x 13"w frt x 12"fl. $235.00.

CHILD'S ROCKER
Ca. 1910; wide pressed top with rare long mushroom-top finials on long stiles; five back spindles, two spindles under arms; only the front stretcher is turned, stretchers on each side and back are plain rounds; pattern-cut arms. 28"h x 13¾"w x 13"dp x 11¾"fl. $135.00.

CHILD'S ROCKING CHAIR
Repainted to original white; seat is heavily scarred — looks like at one time a pressed paper or cloth seat had covered the center; five fanned ball-center spindles with six stick-and-ball shorter ones between the two top down-curved slats — the lowest slat curves up; thick, rounded armrests and their front posts. 31"h. Seat 14"w frt x 12½"w bk x 12"fl. $115.00.

CHILD'S ROCKING CHAIR

All original — dark nut-brown oak stain almost worn off from many years of comfort for the little ones; colorful flowers painted on the Boston Rocker style headpiece almost gone; all parts are of sturdy dimensions — note the legs are socketed onto the rockers. 25"h. Seat 15"w frt x 13"w bk x 10"fl. $195.00.

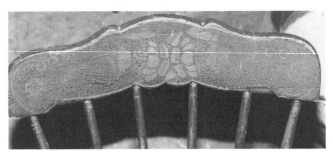

SIDE CHAIR

Formal; restored cranberry red brocade with gimp outline; could be loosely attributed to the Elizabethan Revival style. Ca. 1850s; ornate with carvings, incisings, grooving, spiral twists, and broken pediment; the turned stretcher at center is indicative of quality furniture; deeply carved splat — even the seat frame is patterned. Huge finials. 42½"h. Seat 17"w x 16½"dp. $195.00.

SIDE CHAIR

Black stained with an incised wood seat; broken pediment with heavy carvings; finials; spiral twists; a fancifully designed chair which could only promote sitting with a straight back and feet flat on the floor; note even seat edges are patterned; popular Victoriana. 41"h. Seat 17"w frt x 16"w bk x 18"fl. $250.00 ea set of two.

SIDE CHAIR

Victorian in formal style; gimp edged new upholstery using old patterned cloth; shield (or pineapple) applied carving on wide crest extending out as "crest wings"; tapered front, straight back legs; casters. 38½"h. Seat 17½"w frt x 15"w bk x 17"dp x 16"fl. $225.00.

SIDE CHAIR

Ca. early 1800s; a maker's own ideas from a combination of styles; golden oak; cutout headpiece has a burl inlay; long sticks-and-balls in nine spindles; curved side braces having large knobs; reeded stiles; button turnings; a shallow scalloped apron; incisings; restored caning. A Florida dealer traveling in Pennsylvania noticed pieces of furniture lying beside a county road. He picked up the remains of what seemed to be a chair, and carried them to his car. Upon his return home, with great care and a great deal of time, he was able to achieve the chair's original appearance. It was one of the items in his mall exhibit he somewhat reluctantly put up for sale...but the couple's home was already full of "can't-bear-to-part-withs." 35½"h. Seat 19"widest curve, 18¾"dp x 14½"fl. $225.00.

SIDE CHAIR
Pressed back; new caning; five fanned out spindles; whiplashes and flowers on the crest; stiles end in large flat spool finials; note treatment of stiles' turnings. 40"h. Seat 15"w frt x 14½"w bk x 17'fl. $650.00 set of six.

SIDE CHAIR
Ca. 1890; quarter-sawn veneered seat; hourglass shaped splat; three stretchers at front; side-braced, lightly fanned-out stiles; well-pressed headpiece pattern. 38"h. Seat 16¾"w frt x 16"w bk x 16¼"dp x 17'fl. $350.00 set of four.

BEDROOM CHAIR SET

Oak, plain grain and quarter-sawn; incised
and applied carvings; lyre-shaped center
splat; newly caned seats — more recently
on the rocker; fancy headpiece; turned,
balls, and reeded stiles; the rocker with one
more shaped-edge slat than the straight
chair; the side chair has three turned front
stretchers — this number signifying excellent workmanship. Rocker: 40½"h. Seat 18"w
x 16½"dp x 18"fl/15" when tilted forward.
Chair: 40½"h. Seat 16"w frt x 14"w bk x
16½"dp x 18"fl. $345.00 set of two.

SIDE CHAIR
Golden oak; excellence of workmanship indicated by not only three front stretchers but three at each side, even though not turned; wide pressed headpiece and shaped low slat; seat newly caned as originally; note spiral and ball turnings as well as the unusual stile finials. 34"h. Seat 17"w frt x 16"w bk x 16½"dp x 16"fl. $145.00.

SIDE CHAIR

Dark stained oak; seat center depressed for comfortable sitting; seven plump rounded arrow spindles; shaped crest is deeply impressed with a vase of flowers, laurel wreaths and a small beaded pediment; crest-edging scrolls; stiles top with a button carved over the "bulge." (If there were six the dealer said she would take them home rather than sell them — a favorite of hers.) 39"h. Seat 18"w x 17"dp x 18"fl. $125.00.

SIDE CHAIR

Stained almost black; pressed paper seat with incised pattern; mushroom finials; shell medallion applied to base of the splat, matched by a tiny crest pediment; the excellent workmanship displayed by three front stretchers. (Sales tag on with a thumb tack.) 33"h. Seat 17"w frt x 16½"w bk x 15"dp x 16½"fl. $425.00 set of six.

SIDE CHAIR

Again the three front stretchers telling of skilled cabinetmaking; six shaped spindles with applied simple carvings on wide top headpiece and lower slat; legs taper down into buns. 39"h. Seat 16½"w frt x 15"w bk x 15"dp x 17"fl. $115.00.

SIDE CHAIR
Rush seat; has been painted black; Hitchcock type. Ca. 1830 – 60; pillow shaped handgrip and wide center slat; front turned legs end in bun feet; "ball knees." 34"h. Seat 17"w frt x 16"w bk x 17¾"fl. $95.00.

FIVE SIDE CHAIRS and MASTER'S CHAIR
"Similars" assembled by a dealer at customer's request. Chairs have restored cane seats; wide headpiece and shaped slat; one middle underseat stretcher fastened at plain round side stretchers. Side chair: 40"h. Seat 18"w x 19"dp x 17¾"fl. Host chair: 40"h. Seat 20¼"w x 19"dp x 17¾"fl. $975.00 set of five side chairs and host armchair.

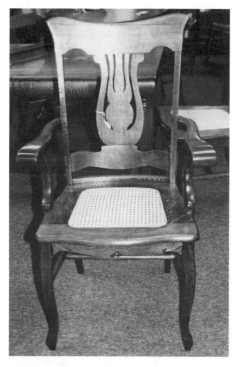

SIDE CHAIRS

Rarely now found as a complete unit; "French" shaped legs; stiles going from the Cherub's Wings headpiece down form the rear legs; good sized curved apron has an unusual tiny inverted pediment at center; lyre back; plain and quarter-sawn. These were advertised in Sears Roebuck's 1908 Catalog as "Outstanding Larkin Co. of Buffalo, N.Y. Chairs." When ordering from Larkin's Catalog, one side chair was given free when two proof of purchase Larkin's Soap wrappers were sent in, and for returning three wrappers to Larkin's, one arm chair was given free. Both chairs were available in either cane or leather seats. Here a Florida antiques shop set up ready for a meal, the set of twelve chairs at a table fully extended. Master's chair: 38½"h. Seat 21"w frt x 17"w bk x 19"dp x 18"fl. Side chair: 38½"h. Seat 18"w frt x 15"w bk x 17½"dp x 18"fl. Extended to its full accommodation (all boards in) the table is 95" long. $225.00 ea chair in set of twelve. Table $835.00.

SIDE CHAIR

Quarter-cut and a little plain cut; the type of chair typically made for dining sets with a table; eye caning restored; applied base-crest and splat-top carvings; rolled piece seatback often seen on these chairs; back legs splayed — those at front serpentine curved. 38½"h. Seat 18½"w frt x 17"w bk x 16½"dp. $895.00 set of four.

SIDE CHAIR

Ca. 1890 – 1900; made by the Larkin Co. (which started as a soap manufacturer and went on to build a huge furniture-making empire at Buffalo, New York); this chair is a standard pattern for Larkin chairs on the Niagara Frontier; the fine three front stretcher workmanship; original eye caned seat replaced with one of plain pressed wood nailed on; seven spindles; attractive deeply pressed crest pattern; acorn finials atop plain and reeded stiles; (hand-braided rag rug type seat pad tied on, $35.00.) 43"h. Seat 18"w x 15½"dp x 18½"fl. $95.00.

97

SIDE CHAIR

On their way to a county auction in Pennsylvania's Lancaster area, dealers heard these called "River Bottom Chairs." Pressed back; plain and quarter-sawn; lovely peacock feathers and center "fan" on wide crest; notice the incised pattern across the lower edge of the seat's apron; three spooled stretchers are evidence of fine quality — principally for their number; shaped center back; pressed paper seat is new. Before and after new seat. 41"h. Seat 18"w frt x 16"w bk x 16½"dp x 17"fl. $625.00 set of four.

SIDE CHAIR
Pressed back; looks like pressing on the lower slat and apron but worn badly; note it has three stretchers. The faded patterns indicate that two adults regularly occupied certain chairs in this set — the other two chairs are in much better condition and may have been seldom used. 40"h. Seat 16¾"w frt x 16"bk x 15"dp x 17"fl. $845.00 set of four.

SIDE CHAIR
Golden oak; simple dignity in the brief turnings; saddle seat; side braces; has a crack at the side of the seat. 38"h. Seat 17"sq x 16"fl. $225.00 set of two.

SIDE CHAIR
Different pressed back of a floral band and beaded and dot frames; two rows of stick-and-ball spindles; side braces; two cutout slats; caning restored; the plain stiles complement the elaborate pressing. 42"h. Seat 18"w frt x 17"bk x 17"fl. $135.00.

MISSION STYLE SIDE CHAIR
Original faded green fabric seat; seven banisters. Originally had been painted green — later stripped for refinishing to a nut-brown oak. The wood's pores (as they almost always do) tenaciously clung to traces of the paint. 36"h. Seat 18"w x 17"dp x 15"fl. $55.00.

LYRE BACK SIDE CHAIR

Ca. 1890 – 1900; pressed back; note the cutout of the splat (related to wooden comb styles that a long time ago were cut in strips like these with one end open); not only are there three of the stretchers at front, but there are also three at each under side; beading on the seat's apron; stiles simply taper at the tops to make the finials; caned seat not original but worn. 40"h. Seat 16"w frt x 13¾"w bk x 14¾"dp x 17"fl. $675.00 set of five.

SIDE CHAIR

High coltish legs; plain and splayed widely at back, turned and straighter at front; delicate pressed medallion in headpiece; note thought put in button and mushroom topped stiles; all other turnings carry out that same idea. 44"h. Seat 15½"w frt x 13½"w bk x 14¾"dp x 21"fl. $185.00.

SIDE CHAIR
Note the wide front stretcher and the three plain turned ones each side; this type not commonly seen; upholstered seat replaces original eye caning. 46"h. Seat 19½"w frt x 16½"w bk x 18"fl. $75.00 ea in a set of six.

SIDE CHAIR
Deeply pressed vase and leaf swirls with many long-spool and button turnings and feet ending in small buns; low back slat step-cut with reeding; stiles are grooved, ending in "rounds" at their tops. 34½"h. Seat 17½"w frt x 16"w bk x 17"fl. $325.00 set of three left from original six.

BENTWOOD CHAIR

("Ice Cream Parlor Chair") Ca. 1920; under-seat original label: "Heywood Bros. & Wakefield Co."; balloon curves. In Fitchburg, Massachusetts, Walter Heywood Co. issued catalogs in 1880's while the Boston grocer Cyrus Wakefield experimented with rattan furniture. 33"h. Seat 16"dia x 18"fl. $65.00.

BALLOON BACK SIDE CHAIR

This is the same style as the ice cream parlor chair except this has side braces and larger curves; both have solid oak wood seats; customarily white oak is used and steamed and pressed while the wood is flexible. 34"h. Seat 17"dia x 18"fl. $75.00.

103

BENTWOOD CHAIR
Impressed letters under the seat: "Fischel Czeck Mrfer"; wood seat has a dimmed stamped pattern; back curved and splayed. 34"h. Seat 15"dia x 18"fl. $65.00 ea — two available.

BENTWOOD LOWBACK CHAIR/STOOL
Center loop back with splayed stiles; curved top slat; a circle firms the legs; the two stiles continuing down from the top to form the legs. 34"h. Seat 15½"dia x 22"fl. $75.00.

SIDE CHAIR

Bentwood style; replacement green vinyl removable seats. Manufacturers still copy Thonet Brother's simple forms. 33"h. Seat 16"dia x 16"fl. $360.00 set of four.

PUB/TAVERN CHAIR

Factory made in the 1800s and shipped all over the country in vast quantities; loop splat; legs splayed and firmed with a curved high stretcher in the round. 34"h. Seat 18"w x 18½"fl. $125.00.

SIDE CHAIR
Slat back; ca. 1870; large-eye restored caning; all four legs are plump, with tapered top and base. 32"h x 16½"w frt x 14"w bk x 17½"fl. $975.00 set of six.

"COTTAGE" SIDE CHAIRS
Found in Maryland — and the wide extended top slat is typical of southern makers; three squared spindles back-curved with fanned-out thick round side posts; a large knot in the seat (usually only wood having small knots was used since the larger ones dried and fell out sooner); splayed rear legs. 32"h. Seat 16"w frt x 14"w bk x 14"dp x 17½"fl. $600.00 set of four.

106

"KITCHEN" CHAIR
Ca. 1910; plank saddle seat; stepdown crest. 32"h. Seat 15"w frt x 13¾"w bk x 16"dp x 16½"fl. $350.00 set of four.

SIDE CHAIR
Ca. 1860; well shaped saddle seat; interesting risers with thinned rounds at the top; vase shaped splat and stepdown sides of the crest. 30"h. Seat 15½"w frt x 15"w bk x 17"fl. $795.00 set of six.

SIDE CHAIR
Manufactured and shipped in great
numbers; plain and quarter-cut oak;
enough turnings and shaping to achieve
sales appeal. 38"h. Seat 16"w frt x 15"w
bk x 15½"dp x 18"fl. $75.00.

SIDE CHAIR
Ca. 1810; note flattened arrowback
spindles, curve of the stiles which,
along with the two back legs, have
darker-stained "bamboo" rings; very
wide splayed legs and a thick saddle
seat. 32"h. Seat 14"w frt x 12"w bk x
15"dp x 17"fl. $195.00.

ARROWBACK "KITCHEN" CHAIR
Plain and quarter-cut; stiles continue from crest into side braces, reinforced with iron rods at the seat; this type iron firms the two front stretchers to the underside of the seat. 38"h. Seat 16½"w. $70.00.

VANITY (DRESSING TABLE) CHAIR
Low back; newly caned seat; golden oak. 28½"h. Seat 15½"w frt x 13"w bk x 18"fl. $125.00.

SIDE CHAIR
Familiar with dining sets; a style from the 1800s carried into the 1900s; quartered and plain cut. 36"h. Seat 15½"w x 17"dp. $95.00 as is; with the addition of the needlepoint seat and necessary padding over the heavy wire base — $225.00.

SIDE CHAIR
Could be an extended family relative with its Windsor characteristics; caned seat restored; fat "knees" either side of seat's narrow curved apron; graceful. 39½"h. Seat 17"w frt x 16"w bk x 15"dp x 18"fl. $125.00.

YOUTH CHAIR
Ca. 1850 – 60; much used at tables; these were often painted — here first a pretty blue, then ending up a white much scarred; restored eye caning; button turned splayed legs and front stretcher; this "Firehouse Windsor" was a popular style in adult and tavern chairs. 26¼"h. Seat 13¼"w x 12"dp. $145.00.

CHILD'S CHAIR
Found in schools, churches, libraries, and wherever children gathered; four baluster back with wide slat top. 29½"h. Seat 13"w x 13"dp x 14"fl. $275.00 set of four.

PRIMITIVE CHILD'S CHAIR
Much used as pull up chairs for the table when tray no longer used; homemade and stained black; woodpegged; carrying or wall hanging slot in back is lower than ordinarily placed; armrests notched to help support the back; wide footrest. 30"h x 14½"w x 16"dp. $68.00.

CHILD'S PRIMITIVE/ "COUNTRY" CHAIR
Simply made with splayed stiles and two slats with nine-slat seat on a firm underpinning of two thick pieces; tapered legs — the stiles forming the two at back. 25"h. Seat 14½"w frt x 12"w bk x 12"fl. $45.00.

SCHOOL CHAIR

Also seen in Sunday school rooms; plain and sturdy, mass produced in great numbers. 29"h x 17"w x 15"dp x 16"fl. $40.00.

SIDE CHAIR

Thick loop back with turned ball and button spindles, front legs, and two stretchers at front; new cane seat. 33"h x 18"w x 17"dp x 17"fl. $175.00 ea — set of five.

SIDE CHAIR
Ca. 1890; original red painted design on the slats is almost obliterated from age and usage; "country" chair from the Shenandoah Valley, all original and in excellent condition. 38"h x 18"w frt x 17"w bk x 18"fl. $2,000.00 set of eight.

SIDE CHAIR
Ca. 1900; sausage turnings and size of ball turnings give this formal chair a robust appearance; three shaped stretchers, while the legs each end in a bun foot. 34"h. Seat 19"w frt x 17"w bk x 17"dp x 18"fl. $725.00 set of six.

Commodes, Washstands, and Dressers

COMMODE
Plain Grand Rapids factory style; besides homes, largely ordered for hotel rooms, at taverns, and boarding houses, to name a few; dull brass knobs; casters; two inside shelves; the generous overhang shelf is typical. 29"h x 31"w x 19"dp. $195.00.

COMMODE
Thick pith rays in the quarter-cutting; wishbone curves support the towel bar; gallery/splashboard is a fancy one; wood-knobbed drawers have factory-type corner dovetails (the dot center scallops); "swell" front doors; at front are large paw feet on dogs' legs while at back are very small paws on straight posts; casters (these furniture pieces usually have wood or iron casters). 53"h x 43½"w x 19"dp. $445.00.

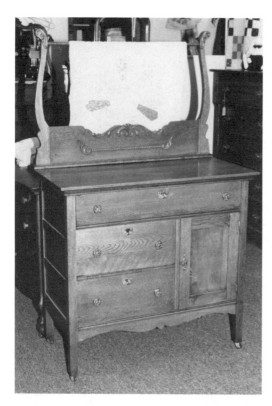

COMMODE
Applied leaf and scroll carvings with a beading length on the uncommonly well-decorated splashboard; carvings at tops of curved uprights; paneled sides; ornamental brass pulls with keykeepers showing all units could have been locked. 58"h x 38"w x 19½"dp. $495.00.

COMMODE
Towel bar between two reeded posts with ball finials (uncommon); stamped elaborate drawer pulls and a small brass knob on the door; bracket feet. 53"h x 30"w x 16"dp. $265.00.

For interest — the typically Victorian Broomfield Chamber Set. These five pieces are from the complete available set of twelve, priced @ $495.00 the set.

VANITY (DRESSING TABLE)
Empire style; convex center drawer, front legs flow with curves into scrolled front feet; back are plain; casters; beveled glass reflects from the three-paneled adjustable wing mirror; four dovetailed corners on each of the drawers. 32"h (mirror center is 24½"h) 38"w x 21"dp. $545.00.

COMMODE
Small splashboard with narrow apron; bowfront drawer; front ledge curved; brass pulls. Wash set for display only. 29"h x 32"w x 19"dp. $135.00.

COMMODE
As found; a good sturdy piece well worth saving — see refinished below. $275.00 as is; $425.00 refinished as planned.

REFINISHED COMMODE
Brass hardware; casters; rolled base at front. A commode differs from a washstand in that it has the inside-door compartment for sanitary accessories. 31½"h x 38"w x 20"dp. $425.00.

COMMODE

Ornate brass pulls and round knob; iron casters; combined woods; typical nineteenth into early twentieth century bedroom piece for metal pitcher and bowl sets, porcelain chamber sets, chamber pots to be kept in area behind the door. Note how pulls are fastened inside after penetrating the drawers. 32"h x 38"w x 20"dp all including overhang top. $495.00.

CHEST OF DRAWERS
Sides and bases of all drawers, as well as the back, are thin pine — a little thicker in the rear; self knobs; and to relieve the squared lines, a slight curve to the apron. 50"h x 30"w x 18¾"dp. $295.00.

CHIFFONIER
Plain and quarter-sawn wood; beveled adjustable mirror held by sinuous posts; thin brass key keepers, keys missing; oversize dovetails on each drawer — the top two are swell front veneered. 72"h x 33"w x 18"dp. $750.00.

CHIFFONIER
Tilting beveled mirror with serpentine uprights; small applied carved pediment; all drawer bottoms are pine; scalloped edge shelf and five-panel sides. 69"h x 30"w x 15½"dp. Top 34"w. $535.00.

CHIFFONIER
Golden oak; fixtures are brass; reverse S-curved posts support wide-beveled tilt mirror. 72"h x 30½"w x 20"dp. $375.00.

PRINCESS BUREAU
Long tilting beveled mirror; low chest has swell front; white china and brass fixtures; short cabriole legs; swan mirror uprights. 72"h x 38"w x 20"dp. $585.00.

PRINCESS BUREAU
Adjustable extra-long beveled glass; brass knob pulls on three dovetailed drawers; simple elegance. 73"h x 40"w x 21½"dp. $585.00.

DRESSER/BUREAU
Wishbone curved sides with applied carvings holding adjustable beveled mirror; stamped brass pulls on two slightly bowed drawers and two longer flat-faced ones, all dovetailed and with keykeepers; original keys lost; scalloped apron and shelfback; pediment carrying out details of other carvings, principally leaf arrangements. 70"h x 48"w x 18"dp. $595.00.

DRESSER/BUREAU
Beveled glass in shield-shaped mirror with a broken pediment; adjustable and held with wishbone sides having delicate applied carvings; brass hardware with keepers on all five storage units — the two smaller drawers with bowfronts. 72"h x 45"w x 18"dp. $585.00.

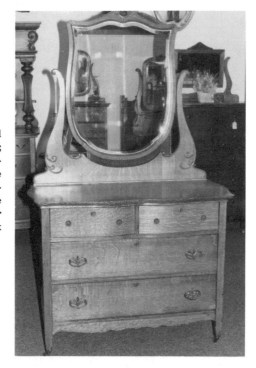

DRESSER/BUREAU

Lavish applied machine carvings on upper posts and crest; scalloped apron; wide beveled tilting mirror; escutcheons on two small drawers and four on wide ones are brass but style differs; all drawers have oak sides and poplar bottoms; paneled sides; wood casters. 82½"h x 42"w x 19"dp. $545.00.

DRESSER/BUREAU

Wishbone frame supports wide beveled adjustable mirror; applied carvings; brass hardware; the bowfront drawers are all mortised fronts with dovetailed back corners; the streak in the crest is in the natural wood and staining to oak browns did not get rid of it. 78"h x 42"w x 20"dp. $635.00.

BUREAU

Half-roll below top (classical Greek style); tilting beveled glass mirror — glass showing some age spots but no harm; five keyholes that once had keys; elaborate brass pulls, the rounds with a center star, the keykeepers fancy; has an air of dignity. 83"h x 49½"w x 22"dp. $795.00.

DRESSER

Applied carvings; leaf pediment; two small front drawers rolled, all having brass fixtures; tilting beveled glass mirror. 72"h x 40"w x 19½"dp. $295.00.

DRESSER

Tilting beveled mirror double oval framed between posts representing the legs and feet with realistic feathers of a mythical monster (probably a griffon, part eagle and part lion, a favorite in decorating for many centuries); all original; a rolled curve tops two small drawers with longer, wider drawers below, all with factory dovetailed corners and quarter-cut veneered fronts; chamfered edges on three sides of top; applied factory moldings extend from the top to form legs with paw feet; a well defined Cupid's head at crest center has a smile and a laurel wreath frame; bronze pulls. 75"h x 47½"w x 24"dp, mirror frame is 43"dia. $935.00.

BUREAU and COMMODE SET
Ca. late 1800s; bow fronts with rounded corners. $1,395.00 the set.

BUREAU
Plain brass knobs on five drawers; all drawer corners dovetailed; tilting mirror which has become marred (an inexpensive piece of mirror glass could be placed behind the present mirror to make it more usable); applied carvings with a shield rolled over the top quartering; a beaded fan and swirls pediment. 80"h x 46"w x 22"dp. $750.00 priced separately.

COMMODE
Matches the bureau; has a towel bar, a splashboard and the original tilting mirror in good condition. 80"h x 40½"w x 22"dp. $685.00 priced separately.

Couches, Pews, and Settees

DEACON'S BENCH/PEW
Ca. mid 1800s; a long church pew was cut down into this shorter deacon's bench; from an upper northwestern New York State church; straight back; each end is full length carved and has a large spool turned post; plain and quarter-sawn oak. 48"l. Seat 13½"dp. $525.00.

CHURCH PEW
(In Missouri several years ago, a member of a congregation made new pews of oak similar to this in style and appealing simplicity.) 40"h x 53"w x 20½"dp 15"fl. $395.00.

COUNTRY-TYPE CHURCH PEW
Golden and dark stained oak finishes; incised cross at each outside panel; note extended width of the seat. 39"h x 57"l x 14¼"dp x 15"fl. $195.00.

CHURCH PEW
Ca. 1890 – 1900; curved seat slopes comfortably back; carvings; paneled sides; finger rolls. 39"h x 55"w x 26"dp x 17"fl. $495.00.

LOVE SEAT and CHAIR SET
Ca. late 1800s; applied carvings with serpentine curves and pediment; cabriole legs at front, plain at back; mustard-gold brocade reupholstered close to the original pattern, with gimp outline. Love Seat: 37½"h x 30¾"w bk. Armchair: 39"h. Seat 21"w x 20"dp. $500.00 set.

FAINTING or PARLOR COUCH
Sometimes placed at the foot of a lady's bed; reupholstered brocade; heavy dark stained oak frame and feet; inside springs construction. 81"l x 30"dp. Head 25"fl. Couch 18"fl. $425.00.

Frames, Mirrors, Pictures, Screens, and Tripod

FIRE SCREEN
Pale golden oak; dragon at center of carved applied shield; spiral turnings and shoefoot base. 29½"h x 19"w. $95.00.

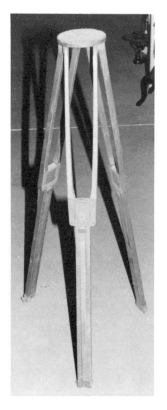

TRIPOD
Very old and not plentiful today; most in private collections and museums; oak and iron with green leather covered top round; screws loosen to adjust height and fold the legs flat. As shown: 39"h. Top 5½"dia. $45.00.

FOLDING SCREEN
Golden oak frame; three sections with the top having many turnings, such as stick-and-ball, whorls, and so on; folds flat; center is higher than the two sides. 70"h. Panels 26"w ea. $195.00.

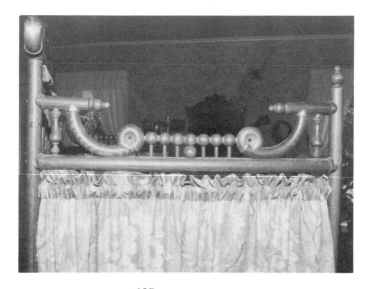

135

FRAME
Gilt liner; 3"w frame; no glass; these widely sought for adding a mirror or picture. 26"h x 19¾"w. $55.00.

PICTURE FRAME
Oval; quarter-sawn; dark stained band with lighter raised beading and wider edge trim. 19½"h x 15½"w. Center oval 12"h x 8"w. Frame only: $165.00.

WALL MIRROR
Plain and quarter-sawn; beveled glass; thick, curved bronze hooks with teardrop tips; applied carvings. 34"h x 38"w. $485.00.

FRAME, PICTURE INCLUDED
Dark stained frame; original painting signed: "R. Hill, 1877"; lilies in delicate vase; thin wood backing; some storage wear. 23½"h x 7"w. $155.00.

Hall Furniture

LIFT TOP BENCH and MIRROR

Bench: The frame on the mirror matches the panel frame on the back of the bench; plain and quarter-cut graceful front legs. Mirror: bronze double garment hooks, each having a lion's head at center with a closed mouth and a formidable expression in the eyes; beveled glass. This set may have been custom made, and so not plentiful in catalogs. Pieces like these required commodious halls — were well liked by the middle class from the late nineteenth into the turn of the twentieth century. Bench: 39"h x 35"w. Seat 18"fl. Mirror: 27"h x 35"w. A rare set; $845.00.

LIFT TOP HALL BENCH
A slight slant forward to the top makes it easier to put fingers under the front edge and lift; a "plain and handsome" bench with "picture frame" type back to relieve the austerity of the bench; front feet have been decoratively firmed with an additional incurved wood piece on each; dealer suggested this had been used in a far northern church first as a deacon's bench. 38"h x 36"w x 14½"dp. $495.00.

HALL (FOYER) STAND

All original; lavishly embellished in spiral turnings; bowed fluted drawer; gilt pulls, bronze hooks; beveled mirror; applied carvings and high finials, a matching finial on the stretcher. 72½"h x 36"w. $1,200.00.

LIFT TOP BENCH

Black stained; a solid looking piece but spared severity by the center back panel; wood pegged sides. Lift top storage well 10"dp. Overall 33½"h x 31½"w x 19"dp. $110.00.

HALL STAND

Dated 1897; an all original piece refinished after having been found encrusted with grime; plain and quartered; lift top seat; iron umbrella hoop but no drip pan; bronze fixtures; unusual split-claw feet at front with plain post feet at back; smaller quartered oak roll at the base of the beveled mirror with a much larger roll at the top; applied carvings on either side of a pediment that is a realistic bust of a goddess — all the features and surrounding head of curls are very well done. 80"h x 36"w x 15½"dp. $2,150.00.

HALL STAND

Mission style; seat top lifts with storage inside; beveled glass; the arches above the mirror complement this example of elegant simplicity typical of mission furniture. At the time of photography, the garment hooks had been removed for cleaning — shown separately below after they were re-installed; black iron. 75"h. Seat 27"w x 16"dp x 18"fl. $565.00.

HALL STAND

With a "wasp waist" and flowing curving lines — in the fashion of ladies' dresses at the time — from the huge Larkin's furniture empire; even the crest is uncommonly graceful; applied carvings; bronze double hat/clothing hooks; a lift top deep seat with a half-scallops apron; wide beveled edge oblong mirror. 72"h x 15½"w x 14"dp. $525.00.

HALL STAND

Lift top seat above deep scalloped apron; overshoes, gaiters, boots, and such outdoor footwear of the period were conveniently stored herein; graceful applied carvings — the lightness carried over to the bronze double hooks; wide-edge beveled mirror. 84"h x 39"w x 17½"dp. $1,095.00.

143

EASTLAKE STYLE HALL STAND

Maker's extra embellishments; newly painted black hoop and brass drip pan, both luckily still intact, for as fashion trends dictated, the hoop was left on or removed; thick rounded button turnings support the arms; incisings and five center sawtooth cuts below seat; instead of a lift top seat here is a drawer with a lovely hollow brass pull; grooved front legs and upper stiles; ornamental brass hat/garment holders. (Sears' 1897 Catalog showed only four hall pieces, all marked their "choicest" in glowing descriptive terms, priced $7.50 to $17.90, 3% discount if paid when purchased with cash in full — no two identical features, though all had the side hoop and drip pan near the floor.) 77"h x 28"w. Seat 13½"dp. $695.00.

EASTLAKE STYLE HALL STAND

Cornice especially typical; roundel at center of high crown pediment with reeded top piece; beveled mirror; burl inlay applied; plain and quarter-sawn; white and gray veined marble shelf with small glass knob drawer; luckily each side retains the original drip pans and iron hoops which accommodated parasols, umbrellas, canes, and the like; three large knob-end wooden pin hooks at each side, customarily only used for hats and lighter capes and such — heavy outergarments might pull over the stand and for that reason, the stands sometimes were permanently anchored to the wall; this narrow flatter armless style customarily found in smaller vestibules and foyers. 82"h. $575.00.

HALL TREE

Ca. early 1800s; large and small turnings; chunky acorn feet on four widely splayed legs; 3"dia cannonball crown; uncommon style. 69½"h. $175.00.

145

Ice Boxes

ICE CHEST
Uncommon size; back has random width boards; two inside shelves; two divided sections for ice and food storage; on brass plate at front just above doors with brass fixtures: "Michigan"; a little extra touch on bracketed type feet. 37"h x 35½"w x 24"dp. $550.00.

LIFT TOP ICE BOX
Brass labeled: "Taylors" in script; galvanized lining; nickel plated iron hardware; note precise joinings of wood pieces each side of the top; front corners rounded. 42"h x 27"w x 18½"dp. $725.00.

ICE CHEST
Black on white metal plate, "Niagara"; ca. 1910; white enameled interior; note attention given to its fine oak construction in the paneling, framing, and bracket base. 44"h x 30"w x 16"dp. $450.00.

ICE BOX
Ca. first quarter of 1900s; brass labeled: "AMERICAN, American Refrigerator Corp., Peru, Indiana"; chrome fittings; interior draining pipe at back. 58"h x 37"w x 21"dp. $895.00.

ICE BOX
Stamped on handles: "Pat, 1900 – 01" Other patents (pending) 1912 through 1919. Label too dimmed to read; brass hardware; back is wood wainscotting; paneled sides. 54"h x 25"w x 19"dp. $575.00.

ICE CHEST
Found in South Australia; dark English oak; underside drip pan; removable wire shelf in lower compartment; metal hardware; centerhole drainage; galvanized ice compartment; now part of an American home. 38"h x 22"w x 16"dp. $285.00.

ICE BOX
Plain and quartered; drip pan behind wood base — removable for emptying; nickel-plated hardware; liftout ice tray for cleaning. 42½"h x 27½"w x 18"dp. $195.00.

Music Makers

VICTROLA
Three metal labels — the first stating where it was sold: "A.H. Mayers — Victrola, 783 Ninth Ave., 1083 Broadway, New York," two others are the maker's customary label: "Victrola (with picture of dog listening to 'His Master's Voice') Talking Machine Co., Camden, New Jersey, U.S.A., Patented in U.S. and foreign countries." Nickel plated fixtures; three wood compartments for needle box next to stand holding records; wood plain and quartered; coffin type lid. The Victrola and cabinet could be purchased separately. The cabinet had a groove into which the Victrola would fit down perfectly. Knobs on Victrolas and base cabinets were set to match exactly in line. The lower doors opening into six shelves have an inside metal catch, as seen in the picture. On original floor models the doors were held by concealed fixtures. $595.00 complete unit. $395.00 Victrola purchased separately.

PUMP ORGAN

Inside back is original paper label: "CLOUGH & WARREN CO., Detroit, Michigan, U.S.A. 1885 – 1887"; elaborately embossed cast iron pedals inside oak frame; round candle shelf is extension of the music rack shelf; concealed metal rollers; handsomely carved 12" long flat handles with fingerholds each side for moving organ about; floral designs; ten original "stops" keys — now one is missing; dealer played the organ to exhibit for interested customers — the tone was beautiful. 49"h x 22" deepest part. $1,200.00 – $1,500.00.

GRAMOPHONE
Ornate case; iron turning handle to activate records is on the right; new front cloth liner; applied dashes, sawtooth, and footed center ornament; lift top; beading below the cloth; note the difference in side posts. 33"h x 24"w x 18"dp. $365.00.

COMMEMORATIVE ORGAN of BECKWITH ORGAN CO.
Chicago; plain and quarter-sawn; commemorates the first English settlement
at Jamestown 300 years after it was established for the "Tercentenary Cele-
bration at the St. Louis, U.S.A. Universal Exposition MCMXVII" — all this on
one of the several paper labels still in excellent condition; both sides have
these paper labels along with the name "Beckwith" embossed on nickel-
plated leaves at two corners. Applied and impressed carvings and reeding;
beveled mirror. 76"h x 40½"w x 23½"dp. $895.00.

SQUARE TOP ORGAN STOOL
Framed leather top which revolves on an iron base, has designed legs and
feet. About 22"h. Seat 14"sq. $135.00.

Details of organ on next page.

The keyboard cover which once could have been locked (key missing) folds up and slides back under the shelf; there are 36 ivory keys, 25 black "sharps and flats," and 11 ivory-front black wooden "pulls."

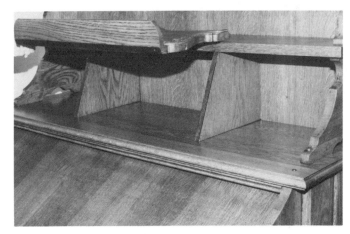

The piano rack, grooved so music will not slip off, folds forwards and up, exposing a third of the two large side compartments for storing music sheets and books.

Foldout wooden knee-operated pedals are above the nickel-plated, iron bound pedals whose once fine velvet tops now have big worn holes in their centers; an egg-and-dart line above the foot pedals.

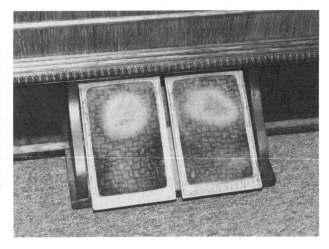

"CONCERT ROLLER ORGAN" (gold letters on top) Five extra rolls, one on machine ready to be played by turning the iron crank with wood handle at lower left — must be manually operated — and it works; wood-knobbed glass window, according to age-yellowed paper label instructions inside, is lifted forward at rear, and folded back; further is printed: "Oil through working parts often; fill the oiler with good sewing machine oil. Keep the instrument in a dry place away from the dust." Iron pull device for insertion of wood cylinder which has tiny brass teeth that carry the notes. 12½"h x 17"w x 14"dp. $1,300.00.

Sewing Machines

SEWING MACHINE Purchased in England by an American family, brought to this country, and well used, but still operable; foot treadle; oak and cast iron; removable cover for liftout machine; red and gold original label: "Jones Family Sewing Machine, Fort Guide Bridge, North Manchester, Eng." 44"l extended. $225.00.

CABINET SEWING MACHINE
Plain and quartered oak; applied carvings; ornate brass pulls; lift top brings up machine — metal fixtures; many storage compartments; iron springs held working machine in place. 31"h x 32½"l x 17½"dp. $375.00.

SEWING MACHINE
"Singer" center of cast iron foot treadle; top lifts and is hinged to afford work space for cloth — this also raising the machine. 31"h x 34"w x 16"dp. $210.00.

SEWING MACHINE
Applied carved letters,
name of maker — "White";
ca. early 1900s; oak with
pine bottom drawers; treadle operated; iron fixtures.
32"h x 34"w x 17½"dp.
$195.00.

PORTABLE ELECTRIC SEWING MACHINE
Patent date: May 27, 1917. Also labeled "Western Electric";
quartered oak veneer case; metal fixtures; completely operable and still has all the extra attachments. 15"h x 19½"w x
9½"dp. $125.00.

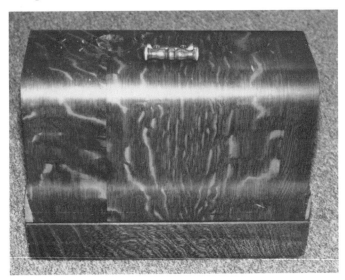

Sideboards and Servers

BUFFET
All original golden oak; lots of character of the staunch oak in its appealing simplicity; beveled mirror; smaller drawers could be locked — those and the larger one all dovetailed at four corners; cutback posts continue into the tapered legs; brass keys are available: mission style. 52"h x 41½"w x 20"dp. $450.00.

BUFFET
Ca. 1890s; round side columns with egg-and-dart at tops; front squared feet having bird claw incisings; six drawers and two doors have pulls made of metallic cords looped around bars; drawers each have thick solid oak sides and rare birds-eye maple bases. 40"h x 60"w x 24"dp. Top overhang is 1½"dp. $495.00.

BUFFET TOP
French style; last owner's usage had been as a wine cabinet, wall hung, braced at base against a small chest; the original buffet bottom was unknown; ten small heavy beveled glass panels form the center door while the same heavy glass is in both narrow high compartments; brass fixtures; heavy applied grooved arched crest molding and fruit arrangement; interesting. 42"h. $325.00.

163

TOP OF A BUFFET

Oak runs the gamut from the simplicity of country furniture, through moderate and excessive ornamentation, into the elegance portrayed in this piece — always maintaining its substantial dependability. This is without a base, at least no base was ever known to the dealer who bought it in an estate sale — where it had for years been used as an impressive dining room side cabinet. There are iron wires on the back for wall hanging. Brass escutcheons; the original keys are available; brass hinges; incised, carved, and applied carvings, including sawtooth rows, stick and ball, a gallery with outstanding finials, and elegant posts at the shelf sides and forming the legs in front of a miniature stick-and-ball row at the base. Note particularly the elaborate escutcheons and the oval framed bonneted busts of girls facing each other, each surrounded by scrolls, leaf, and floral carvings. 56"h. Top shelf 46½"w. Bottom shelf 43½"w. Top 15"dp. Bottom 13"dp. $450.00.

BUFFET

Half-rolls divide glass into three sections in the two upper doors, while the center mirror is beveled glass; replacement china knobs and original brass escutcheons, hinges and lost keys; there is a brown veined marble shelf. Note side posts and the roll at the base of the solid wood doors center frame. 73"h x 46"w x 18¾"dp. $1,095.00.

SERVER

Ca. 1930; factory dark-stained oak and maple; had even been used as a child's dresser; original beveled glass stained; small scallop-edge crest; six self-wood knobs pull open grooved and dovetailed drawers; three shelves inside paneled doors; bracket feet. 32¾"h x 23¾"w x 8½"dp. $195.00.

BUFFET
Empire revival style; varied-size dove-tailed drawers; one shelf inside to accommodate both doors; beveled mirror; 2½" to 4" thick curved shelf-side supports, the theme followed in roll between doors and the side posts flowing into the front feet; plain back feet are an extension of the back frame — all with casters. 55"h x 48"w x 22"dp. $585.00.

166

HALF and HALF
(Combined china cabinet and sideboard.) Rare furniture piece; plain and quarter-cut wood; full length convex glass door, one full side and shelf-level glass at shelf with beveled mirror; brass fixtures; bow front drawer is felt-lined for silver storage; side lamp shelf; two shelves behind solid doors; applied carvings and flutings with a griffin (a mythical half-eagle, half-lion monster) at each side on buffet and a heavy pediment at center of that crest; a high galleried side; three shaped front feet and three plain at rear have wood casters. 68"h x 48"w x 19"dp. $1,895.00.

SERVER
Nut-brown stains to original when refinished; wide drawer with wood knobs is dovetailed; the gallery is 3" high widening to 4" at center; straight legs shaping into dog's legs and feet at the front, remaining plain to the floor at the back; wide shelf. 37"h x 36"w x 18½"dp. $425.00.

SIDEBOARD
(Lowback buffet styles generally later than the taller sideboards;) self-wood knobs and brass fixtures, including a keykeeper to lock the center door; shelf behind center door has three round holes for wine bottle storage; graceful arched crest with an open-mouth lion's head at each side; ½"dp beveled mirror; applied carvings with a formal air; lion's claw feet; dovetails on the drawer's corners. 52"h x 48"w x 22"dp. $1,195.00.

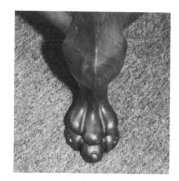

SIDEBOARD
Bowfront with lots of storage space; serving or display shelf whose turned and fluted short pedestals support a high gallery with an applied pediment and side s-curves; beveled mirror; five keykeepers (keys lost); slat-paneled sides; casters. 74"h x 50"w x 20"dp. $1,185.00.

SIDEBOARD
Uncommonly high gallery with unusual carved finial extensions of the reeded stiles; brass pulls and escutcheons on each of the three drawers and two doors, incisings and carvings; casters; five slim brass rods with wood sides enclose each end of the middle shelf; large turnip feet. 75"h x 50"w x 22½"dp. $795.00.

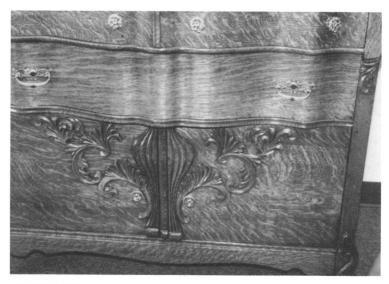

SIDEBOARD

Bits and pieces too lovely not to show even though it was impossible to get the picture in its entirety because this delivery of furniture from the dealers' refinishing warehouse was not yet properly placed in the shop. Beveled mirror; extensive embellishments — carved, applied carvings, moldings even applied swirls on the castered front feet, those at back plain; brass fixtures with a fluted carving half on each side of the center door post; bowfront drawers. 74"h x 50"w x 24"dp with the extra-wide center shelf. $1,095.00.

SIDEBOARD

(One of the taller sideboards, which are generally earlier than the lowback servers/buffets;) note the thick tiger quartering on the bow-front drawers; beveled glass mirror; fluted posts support the carved swans holding the galleried shelf; typical hollowback stamped brass fixtures and keyhole escutcheons — five inside storage units could all be locked; paw front feet — plain at back — all with wood casters. 72"h x 48"w x 22"dp. $725.00.

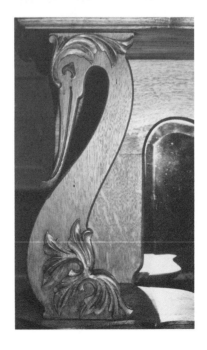

Tables

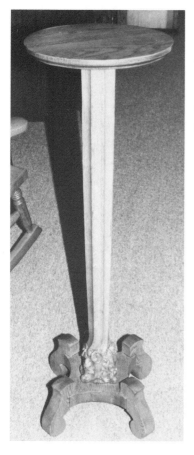

CANDLESTAND
Ca. 1910; flower cluster carvings at the bottom of a heavy post; darker stained feet; base has four concave sides. 37"h. Top 12½"dia. $295.00.

CANDLESTAND
Ca. 1910; cannonball on an inverted cup at bottom of post; darker stains below; thick rays from quarter-cutting. 37"h. Top 12½"dia. $295.00.

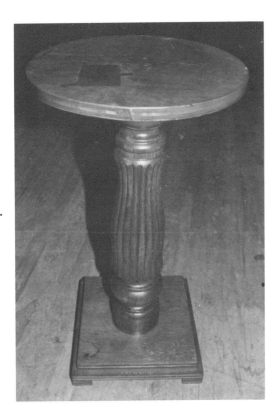

PEDESTAL/TABLE
Fluted stem; veneered top.
27½"h. Top 15"dia. $45.00.

**SALESMAN'S SAMPLE
PEDESTAL/TABLE**
Always a delight to find one of these
today; repainted with two shadings
of the original "wagon green." 12"h.
Top 11"dia. Base 10"w. $185.00.

TABOURET/ JARDINIERE STAND (regional names) Ca. 1850; plain and quarter-cut; top has concave edges. 29"h. Top 19"sq. $140.00.

PLANT STAND/RACK
Homemade with brass "saucer" in which a pot of ferns or flowers might be placed (here it holds a "conversational" chunk of Lake Ontario driftwood); primarily oak, with a pine leg repair. 25½"h x 10"sq. $65.00.

STAND/TABLE
Scalloped top edge; cabriole legs; narrow apron. 17"h. Top 14"dia. $185.00.

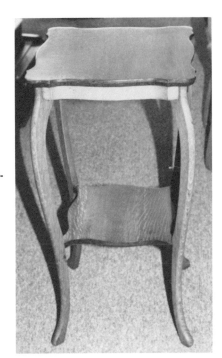

FERN STAND
Ca. 1875; splayed legs to help withstand weight of the plant (for which this stand had been used for several generations); narrow apron with a decorative cutting at each corner below the overhanging table top. 18"h. Top 18"sq. Lower shelf 6"sq. $125.00.

STAND /TABLE
Many usages — one being typewriter table as displayed on shop sales tag. Plain top and shaped lower shelf; spool and flat button turnings with small ball feet. 30"h. Top 16"sq. $75.00.

STAND/TABLE
Sausage turned legs with ball feet; table sides slope into a narrow apron; shelf edges curved. 30"h x 24½"sq. Shelf 16"sq. $265.00.

STAND/TABLE

Button and spool turnings with scallops and a deep edge grooved top make this table beautifully constructed; type used in hundreds of parlors for (primarily) family bibles. Below could be a stereoptican with a box of views or an illustrated book of bible stories. 29½"h. Top 24"sq. Shelf 16"sq. $245.00.

CHILD'S TABLE
"Backyard project" made with care; ca. 1900. 17½"h x 20½"l x 12½"dp. $28.00.

FERN STAND
Applicable for other usages, and since the early 1900s, probably was so applied. 18¾"h x 13½"rd. Lower shelf 9½"dia. $125.00.

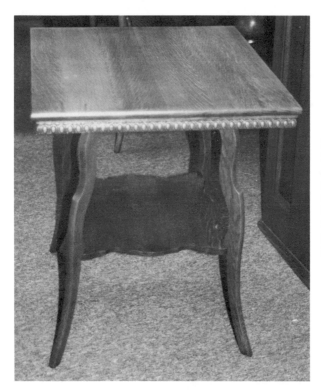

CENTER/PARLOR TABLE
Apron with egg-and-dart pattern; curved, splayed legs; deeper stained shelf. 28½"h. Top 24"sq. Shelf 17"sq. $225.00.

TABLE/STAND
Turned splayed legs end in small claw-and-glass-ball feet. 29"h. Top 24"sq. Shelf 16"sq. $175.00.

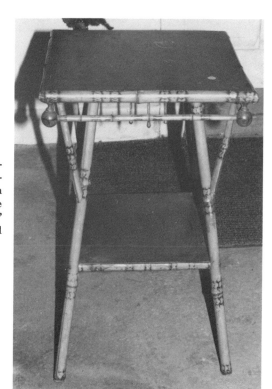

STAND/TABLE
Oak top and shelf with bamboo; birdcage apron; bamboo was greatly used here in furniture making — cane being our native "bamboo" — especially in spindles and legs. 29"h. Top 18"sq. $75.00.

SHELVES/WALL RACK
Sturdy oak shelves with bamboo. 13"h x 10"w x 7"dp. $28.00.

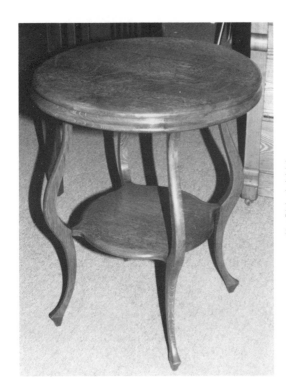

PARLOR TABLE
Layered top; cabriole legs; this Queen Anne style was popular in many sizes. 30"h. Top 24"dia. Shelf 15"dia. $295.00.

STAND/TABLE
Ca. 1850s; bamboo framing oak; legs braced into underside of tabletop. (Woods such as maple and pine were sometimes turned to imitate bamboo). 29"h. Top 19"sq. Shelf 10"sq. $140.00.

DINING TABLE
An extra board extends seating space; large ball feet on quarter-cut legs with bell cups; serpentine style stretchers provide additional stability; two center posts separate when table is pulled open for extension. 29"h x 47½"dia. $325.00.

DINING TABLE
Chairs placed for shop display only; this has three extra leaves that fit in when the table is pulled apart. 30"h. Top 48"dia. $835.00.

DINING TABLE
No leaves available; extra-heavy ball turned and octagonal center post; plain and quarter-cut; wood casters; most tables in this book have either the original wood or iron casters, or replacements; narrow apron; sometimes on the old tables, the apron is so wide it is difficult to find chairs with seats low enough. 30"h x 42"dia. $645.00.

DINING TABLE
Good "fire" (glowing natural finish); no extra leaves available but no indication it could be extended; very large lion's paw feet with carved hair at the sides. 29"h x 42"dia. $645.00.

DINING TABLE

Ca. 1880 – 90; quarter-cut table "takes" eight
12"w each leaves; on extension tables, extra
leaves are a big plus because through the
years leaves were lost, damaged or warped, or
were diverted to another table of the same
dimensions. Arches that support the legs and
the center posts, as well as the necessarily
heavy legs and feet, are all elegantly turned
with carvings — the spiraled acanthus leaves
are one of the Empire styles borrowed from
ancient Greek excavations. Table 30"h x 47"sq.
$850.00. The chairs used with this table are
newly caned, with many turnings. 42"h x
17¼"w frt x 15¾"w bk x 17½"fl. $750.00 set of six.

DINING TABLE
Solid top; Pennsylvania piece; plain and quarter-sawn wood; a ring around the thick post; cutout base with four curled feet having casters. 33"h x 48"dia. $835.00.

DINING TABLE
Ca. 1890; plain and quarter-cut golden oak; 4"dp apron; attractive groove-framed base and over-size lion's paw feet; casters; this table was made for extension but no leaves remain with it. (The realistic claws/toenails on these big animal feet never ceased to fascinate me as I was photographing.) 30"h x 48"dia. $1,045.00.

DINING SET

Table: Uncommonly large legs at corners of square table and under at center; plain and quartered wood; iron casters; five extra original leaves for extending table length. 30"h x 42"sq.

Chairs: Each has pressed headrest and bottom slat; side braces from seat to stiles; spool turned spindles; note finials of flat buttons and mushroom tops; turned tapered legs ending in ball feet; front stretchers' turnings match spindles in chair back; side and rear stretchers plain rounds; new caning in the seats. 33"h x 16"w frt x 14"w bk x 16"fl.

$1,740.00 the set, if sold separately: table $845.00, the five chairs $895.00.

185

TABLE
Widely scalloped edges
with applied carvings;
plain and quartered;
veneered top. 30"h x
24"sq. Shelf 20"sq.
$295.00.

TABLE
Stickley made ca. 1940; poplar top on oak; barley twist legs. 29"h x
39"sq. $450.00.

PARLOR/ OCCASIONAL TABLE
Quartering exposed these unusually vivid pith rays in a fantasy of shapes making up the top with its narrow beading-edged apron and shelf. These tables were part of the bric-a-brac and furniture-filled rooms of the Victorian period; pad foot type. 29"h. Top 24"dia. $265.00.

PARLOR TABLE
Plain and quarter-cut; brass eagles' claws and glass-ball feet, such feet in the largest sizes commanding high prices; claws holding wooden balls are rarely seen — and maintain a still higher value. 27½"h. Top 27¾"dia. Shelf 16"sq. $385.00.

PARLOR TABLE
Golden oak; note legs and supports of the lower shelf 13"dia.
29"h. Top 20"sq. $215.00.

ACCENT TABLE
(Name often used by dealers.)
4-leaf clover lower shelf; scallop
edge chamfered top. 29"h. Top
17¼"sq. Shelf 11"sq. $155.00.

TABLE
Golden oak with lightweight brass design on all four legs; clover-leaf styled top with scalloped shelf. 30"h. Top 24"widest part. Shelf 14"w. $225.00.

PARLOR TABLE

A most fanciful theme of flowing graceful lines; top partially quarter-cut, rest of table is plain-cut; note apron blocks, beading, and flaring cutouts of shelf sides. 30"h. Top 22"sq. Bookshelf 18"sq. $265.00.

LIBRARY TABLE

Empire style; oval; five-paneled top; plain and quarter-cut wood; top laps over apron by 1½"; very heavy octagonal posts. 29½"h x 42"oval length x 26½"widest part. $365.00.

LIBRARY TABLE
Solid oak with a "no-nonsense" look; two brass ring pulls on drawer; appealing in solid oak with its columned posts and "knuckle" feet. 30½"h x 41½"l x 26"w. $185.00.

LIBRARY TABLE
Plain and quartered; grooved apron; brass knob on drawer. 30½"h x 40½"l x 24"w. $195.00.

LIBRARY TABLE
Plain and quarter sawn; stretchers; beading; wide apron; small dogfeet ending curved legs. 34"h x 42"l x 24"dp. $145.00.

LIBRARY TABLE
Ca. 1890; golden oak; pressed pattern on veneered drawer front opened by inserting fingers under scallop; mortised construction. 28"h x 40"l x 24½"dp. $295.00.

LIBRARY TABLE
Different grains in six-board top; quartered rolled
apron; dovetailed drawer on one side pulled out by
inserting fingers under apron; reeded and turned
legs and feet. 28½"h x 42"l x 26"w. $535.00.

Trunks

SALESMAN'S TRUNK
Brass plate inside lid with black paper covering reads:

Established 1850
J. R. Hughes & Co.
Manufacturers of
Trunks, Traveling Bags, and Umbrellas
Salesroom, 40 North High Street
Telephone No. 497   Columbus, Ohio
Sample Trunks a Specialty

Oblong, all original and mint condition; many compartments of various sizes inside for sample wares; brass plated iron and blackened iron fixtures; nailheads fasten top-securing leather bands; all edges protected by the leather held decoratively at front with iron "butterflies"; large brass key in lock. 13"h x 40"w x 20"dp. $225.00.

FLAT TOP TRUNK
Punched on the brass hasp is: "Yale & Towne Mfg. Co. Stratford, Conn. U.S.A." Inside the lid looks like a squarehead horseshoe nail was used to punch initials "CD" (which the owner might have added); fanciful but practical leather trim and reinforcements, nailheads, beading, and iron; inside side-ledges meant to hold a now-missing tray; handsome escutcheon but key long gone. 26"h x 38½"w x 23"dp. $225.00.

FLAT TOP TRUNK
Iron bands typical on these types much used for travel, getting banged about on stage coaches, oxen or horse-drawn wagons and prairie schooners, in baggage cars on trains, even sea voyages; leather handles; large escutcheon framed a center keyhole for locking; key missing. 21"h x 32"w x 18½"dp. $125.00.

DOME TOP TRUNK
Blackened iron and wood strips on the oak; could be locked and further kept tightly closed with the side latches; excellent condition; found in Maryland. Lid is open to show remains of a typical picture of the 1800s — of a pretty girl; would be a shame (I think) to scrape it off. 18"h x 27"l x 14¾"dp. $165.00.

NAVAL BOX (SEA TRUNK)
English oak; recently painted black, with British naval symbols on the front, seascape on top; flat side plates hold iron handles; inside a 4" wide box the full trunk width held personnal items (while customarily these in American trunks, especially when bought for northern usage, held pine cones as insect deterrents); becoming much sought in our country for home furnishings. 18"h x 37½"w x 20½"dp. $695.00.

DEED BOX
Ca. 1870 – 80; deep, slightly rounded lid; handsome brass trim; leather straps and carrying handle; black iron hasp and key escutcheon; white lined. 10½"h x 24½"w x 6"dp. $245.00.

GUN CHEST
Ca. 1870; homemade in western Kentucky; iron handles; brass fasteners holding heavy wood bands; now-faded original black paint; lift top. 17"h x 37"w x 16"dp. $185.00.

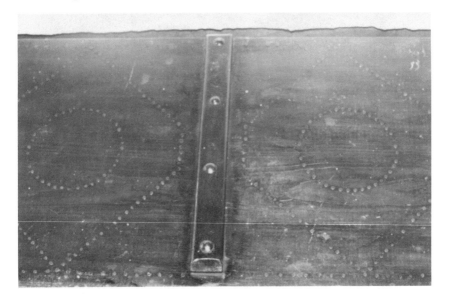

DOME TOP TRUNK
Original red paint now scarred and faded; tin veneered oak base; three grooved wood trim strips secured by dulled brass fingers; two flip-up latches hold down top with larger ornamental one at center which held a key now broken off; four underside iron rollers; original leather handle each side. 23"h x 32½"w. $135.00.

DOLL'S TRUNK
Simulated leather paper; light oak strips and black painted fixtures; heavy latch for this type trunk. 7¾"h x 14"w x 7¾"dp. $45.00.

RARE SQUARE FLAT TOP called a "FANCY TRUNK" Patented July 1, 1873; punched dot patterns on two wide metal bands reinforcing sides and top; iron fingers hold each end of wood strips; two iron latches clasp down lid while a leather flap covers top of brass latch having original key; deep lid permits stashing therein; inside, this "false top" has at center a faded picture of a lady in a period gown; worn paper lining; four underside concealed iron rollers. 21"h x 30"w. $155.00.

DOME TOP TRUNK
Plain blackened iron bands; iron fingers holding wood strips; leather adjustable to secure top. While dome tops give more storage space inside, flat tops are much in demand as chairside tables and such. 19"h x 30"w x 17"dp. $170.00.

And More

FIREPLACE MANTEL — EMPIRE STYLE
A huge one in quarter-sawn oak; columns with rolled fronts on square bases with grooved trims; same type columns at either side of the beveled mirror; gallery tops a wide shelf. 96"h x 58"w x 12"dp. $895.00.

HOME MEAT LOCKER (ICE BOX)
Made from oak in England, carried to an Australian home then purchased and brought to an American home, converted in usage to a silver/linen cabinet. An interesting, rare "box" with its clear, green, and amber leaded glass panels in unique designs; a diamond shaped mirror on the center door; ice originally kept in left compartment; iron fixtures are all nickel-washed. 66"h x 54"w x 15½"dp. $1,800.00 in a 1985 professional appraisal.

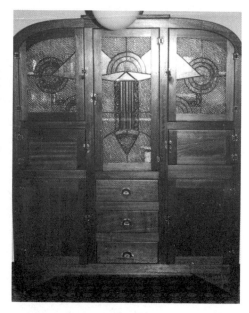

SPINNING WHEEL
Small size that could be easily moved about — more desirable than the very large heavier ones; front legs are splayed 22" apart; primitive homemade base; spool and button turnings with the legs ending in shaped feet. Seldom are these now found with the original distaff — the word coming from Anglo-Saxon "dis" for bundle of flax and "stoef" for stick. The distaff, made by the local woodworker, or from a suitable branch cut and bent to the correct shape, held the fibers ready to be spun into thread. Overall 51"h incl. distaff. Center 33"w. Thick board is 7"w. $485.00.

TELEPHONE
Ca. 1918; can be attached for operation; wall hanging style; brass label: Stromberg Carlson; adjustable mouthpiece, brass double bells and a side turn handle; earpiece rests in a slot on the other side. 19"h x 8"w x 5½"dp. $400.00.

THE "OAKS" or KITCHEN CLOCK
Octagonal wood frame; brass ring is opened by a thin tiny bar for entry under the glass face to key-wind the eight-day time and striking movements inside the case; marked with a now-faded "Ingraham" — topmost among clock manufacturers ca. 1890 – 1915; fancy brass pendulum swings behind bottom glass with "Regulator" in gold paint; wall hanging. 24"h x 16½"w x 6"dp. $165.00.

POSTMASTER'S CLOCK
Ca. late 1800s; fluted dark stained oak case;
round brass pendulum and pull chains for
adjusting; wood weights; high up on the
kitchen wall of a far north collector's home.
12"dia. $250.00.

**KITCHEN CLOCK (GINGER-
BREAD CLOCK)**
Spring operated; original
paper label on back unread-
able; ornate brass pendulum;
glass door inside decorated;
elaborate trim on oak case;
has key. 23"h x 13"w x 6"dp.
$165.00.

BARBER'S BRUSH
Or could have been used in a clothing store, by tailors, in a gentleman's dressing room; oak handle; an interesting collectible that could be termed an accessory. 13½"l x 4"w. $22.00.

DOLL'S BUGGY
Only the top was restored with new material; all else is original — dark red painted oak with mustard yellow striping; woven reeds; cloth lined; black iron double handle with wood grip and spring carriage base with the metal wheels. 36"h x 11½"w x 33"l. $325.00.

COASTER WAGON
All original, painted in now-faded mixed colors; on side: PIO-
NEER Artillery wheel COASTER; oak and hickory; iron fix-
tures; note brake at side. 13"h x 32"l x 13"w. $495.00.

CHILD'S SPRING ROCKING HORSE
Ca. 1930; heavy oak with iron springs and fixtures; note
expression of the eyes. 29"h x 36"l. $145.00.

SMALL CHILD'S PUSH SLEIGH
Ca. late 1800s; all original red painted, mustard yellow striped oak; black 15"w handle bar; parents could push while walking about — or even when parents were ice-skating; iron bound wood runners; deep sides. 23½"h. $295.00.

BOBSLED
All original; oak and birch; painted. 74"l x 12"w. $375.00.

PULL SLED Stamped: "Made By PARIS MFG. CO. South Paris, Me., U.S.A." Letters AO (probably owner) painted on underside; iron bound oak runners. 26"l. Seat 9"w. $225.00.

MILK SLED
For deliveries; ca. 1890; iron bound runners and ring at the front bar through which a pull-rope was tied; still good dark green paint. 47'l x 19½"w. $175.00.

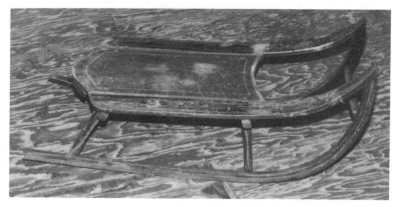

CHILD'S PULL SLED
Pulled with a hemp rope; original red and "wagon green" paint; iron bound oak runners; curved-up front. 32"l x 12"w. $225.00.

WORK SLED
Short iron bars front reinforcements; used to haul small logs, firewood, buckets of coal, children for fun — whatever needed to be carried. 48"l. $145.00.

SLED
Homemade about 1875; one wood strip broken; could have been rope pulled, or from wear signs might have been carried underarm as the person ran — then rushed to the ground and flopped down upon for coasting. 48"l. $100.00.

WORK SLED
Ca. late 1800s; backyard project; front bar for attaching rope. 47½"l. $100.00.

SNOWSHOE CHAIR
Oak with natural hide strips and brass; an oval brass plate at the back; "W.F. TUBBS CO., SNO SHU CHAIR, NORWAY, ME. USA"..."Patent appld. for" date is obliterated with age. Has a pair of snowshoes imprinted as their trademark. 25½"h x 14"w. Seat 19"dp. $250.00.

STORE COUNTER PAPER ROLL HOLDER
Roll not included in price; oak and iron; permanently fastened to store counter; paper cutting guide embossed: "REX" with side trims and "24" at each end. Again, as is so often happening, these once in good supply in the marketplaces, now are seldom seen in the original, and in usable condition. 12"h x 29"w. $125.00.

CASH REGISTER
Label: "Inspected by John Blank, Mar. 4, 1906"; also, "NAT'L. CASH REGISTER CO. Dayton, O. USA F.B. PATTERSON, PRES."; glass, brass, white marble shelf; key is available that opened the cylinder front covering keys' operation; flip-up registering numbers; placed in an oak case; thought to have been used for many years in a Pennsylvania barber shop. Register itself is 17"h x 17"w x 16"dp. Overall with case 26½"h x 22½"w x 22"dp. $795.00.

STORE WHOLESALE TEA BOX

Covered oak box; top and four sides with elaborate designs and lettering in red, brown, and off-white; hinged top with a brass ring-pull; labeled: "MONOGRAM, Panpipe Japan Tea, Imported by SMITH, PERKINS & CO., First of the New Crop." 19¾"h x 16¼"w. $90.00.

END of SHIPPING BOX

These advertising parts of old containers are popular wall decor and values increasing; in black paint is: "MEDICINES, The J.R. Watkins Company, From Ocean to Ocean, New York, N.Y., Chicago, Ill., Boston, Mass., Newark, N.J., Columbus, O., Kansas City, Kan., Winona, Minn., Memphis, Tenn., Oakland, Cal., Montreal, PQ, Hamilton, Ont., Winnipeg, Man., Vancouver." $12.00.

FRUIT PRESS

Once in regular use on north-western New York's Niagara Frontier; oak and hickory; red paint with yellow trim still good; iron handhold to manually turn crushing device inside wood slat barrel; iron fixtures; a very heavy collectible but interesting in a home or office. 40"h x 20"w x 14"dia. $225.00.

BUTTER CHURN
From a Large Great Lakes Dairy Operation

Ca. 1870; oak and iron; red stain still fine; staves construction; drainage plug; cracked wood top has an "eye" to observe status of churning going on in the barrel; also a metal plate on the top; labeled: "Wortman's, Manufacturers, London, Ontario"; can be moved about. 20"h. Barrel 18"dia. $185.00.

CAROUSEL PONY
White base and brilliant colors in hand painting on oak — all original; age and usage make joinings more apparent. These have become much sought among decorators and buyers wanting unusual furnishings. 55"h. $650.00.

PEDESTAL TOP HORSE
A very early carving from oak — probably when the wood was green; oriental influence; these fit into many room and office settings. 33"h x 31½"l nose to tail. $375.00.

Glossary

acanthus — design taken from the leaf of a southern European plant, based in archaic architectural forms, revived in the nineteenth century

apron — a trim or structural aid at the base of seats, cabinet forms, and the like

bracket foot — a triangular base for the support of cased (enclosed) pieces

burl — knotty growth on hardwood and semi-hardwood trees of the best quality, such as oak, maple, ash, with a knotty grain; thinly sliced, it is highly regarded as veneer for fine furniture

cabriole — curved tapering leg used as early as the 1600s and re-applied in the nineteenth century; many variations in both legs and feet

casters — small rollers set into the feet or furniture bases to facilitate moving the piece about; dealers often replaced these in wood or iron — hopefully to match the originals

chamfer — a beveled or grooved edge

dovetailing — a joint made by interlocking wedge-shaped tenons and mortises, as the corner joints of drawers. "Dovetailing" named for its likeness to the tails of doves. A factory style one might notice on old pieces today resembles scallops with center dots, as children's hightop shoes that had the buttonholes placed in the center of the scallops so that the buttons would sit in the scallop centers.

ebonize — to simulate ebony; to stain or paint black

emboss — decorations raised from a surface

escutcheon — decorative plate around a keyhole

finger roll — hollowed out continuing concave rolls cut into the margins of a chair, settee, and such

finial — terminal piece, plain or ornate, such as an acorn, figural, or urn

fluting — semicylindrical channels or grooves, as in a column

gallery — a fretwork for solid decorating, or as a railing around tops or shelves of furniture forms

gimp — narrow fancy trims around fabrics, as in upholstery

incising — surface designs often deeply cut

inlay — decorative patterns or designs of contrasting materials set into the surface of an object

mortise (and **tenon**) — the mortise is the cavity or cut into which the tenon is fit, the tenon first being cut and shaped for insertion; (huge such corners noted on a Georgia barn built 149 years ago — and still holding together)

pediment — ornamental structure topping a cased piece; **broken pediment** — one interrupted with a separate crest

reeding — convex moldings resembling natural reeds; the opposite of **fluting**

roundel — a furniture term meaning any round or circular ornament

slat — a thin, flat, narrow piece of wood used to brace the back of a chair

splat — a thin, broad piece of wood forming the center vertical piece in a chair back

stretcher — horizontal bracing on the underside of a table or chair

stiles — upright elements in frames; the side supports of chair backs

veneer — thin layer of choice wood or various other materials glued upon a commoner surface for ornamentation

whorl foot — upturned scroll, a **knurl**

Index

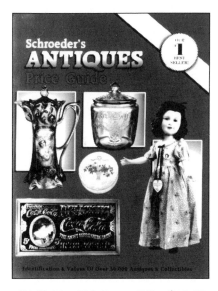